200 Ways to RAISE a Girl's Self-Esteem

An Indispensable Guide for Parents, Teachers & Other Concerned Caregivers

Will Glennon

Foreword by Virginia Beane Rutter

CONARI PRESS
Berkeley, California

Conari Press books are distributed by Publishers Group West.

Cover design by Ame Beanleand

Cover photo by Marie McEnery

Book design by Claudia Smelser

Library of Congress Cataloging-in-Publication Data
Glennon, Will, 1949—

    200 Ways to raise a girl's self-esteem : an indespensable guide for parents, teachers, and other concerned caregivers / Will Glennon ; foreword by Virginia Beane Rutter.

       p.   cm.

    Included bibliographical references

    ISBN: 1-57324-154-7 (trade paper)

1. Girls—psychology. 2. Self-esteem in children. 3. Self-esteem in adolescence. 4. Parent and child. 5. Teacher-student relationships. I. Title

HQ777.G6 1999	99–24222
649'.133—dc21	CIP

Printed in the United States of America on recycled paper

99 00 01 02 03 DATA 10 9 8 7 6 5 4 3 2 1

200 Ways to Raise a Girl's Self Esteem

Foreword: Herstory in the Making

In classical Greece, the virgin goddess Artemis was the patroness of young girls. Greek girls prayed to Artemis, asking her to delay their menarche. Until a girl had her first period, she was considered to be a wild, untamed female; with the onset of menarche, she would become a woman who could then be subdued by marriage. Because marriage meant childbearing and the high risk of a young mother's death in childbirth, girls feared entering adulthood. As their bodies began to change in their prepubescent years, many experienced intense anxiety and emotional disturbances. Some girls even attempted suicide by hanging themselves.

With the onset of puberty, Greek girls gradually adjusted to their fate, beginning with a special ceremony in which they offered their childhood clothes to Artemis, sacrificed their "girlhood," and then moved on to assume their new responsibilities without resistance. They continued to ask for Artemis' protection and blessing on first pregnancies and childbirth and were slowly integrated into the community of young adults.

Tragically, like classical Greek girls who prayed to Artemis, our daughters also resist their changing bodies as they move toward puberty. Not only have mothers and fathers traditionally turned away from this sign of their daughters' development, but everything in the media tells girls that they are now objects of shame and must hide or camouflage themselves. The natural weight gain that girls experience at puberty is insulted by the ubiquitous ideal of a Barbie-doll shape and incessant diet fads in teenage girls' magazines. Above all, girls in adolescence are at risk for unwanted attention from men. Not only does a girl have to assume the self-care of a menstruating young woman, but she has to be aware of defending herself against sexual advances at a very young age.

Our cultural expectations of girls becoming women have had a similar psychological effect. Although our daughters are not expected immediately to marry, give up their identities, and have children, they instead are faced with giving up their core selves and dissembling their strengths in order to be accepted. Girls are hurting themselves to release feelings of frustration and to affirm their own aliveness. Anorexia and bulimia are likewise rising in girls at alarming rates. At their extreme, these are suicidal behaviors. Many of our daughters are unconsciously reenacting the myths surrounding the goddess Artemis as they become women.

The explosion of attention to girls' drop in self-esteem at adolescence promises to change these archaic, deeply embedded attitudes that undermine girls' development. But our daughters need more than techniques with which to fight off aggressors. They need caring adults to teach, advise, and create rituals that help girls negotiate the transition to a whole, multidimensional womanhood that is based on feminine values but also includes roles traditionally thought to be male.

This book refreshingly offers a man's voice raised on behalf of girls. Author Will Glennon, father of a grown daughter, brings his own perspective to the tenets that have emerged in the research on girls in the last ten years. In this manual, he outlines in a straightforward way the principles for raising healthy girls and suggests exercises for both parents and teachers. A practical guide, *200 Ways to Raise a Girl's Self-Esteem* can be used both at home and in schools. Glennon contributes one more strong voice to those lobbying for girls' selfhood, a selfhood based on being woman-identified, instead of male-identified—herstory in the making.

—Virginia Beane Rutter, Jungian analyst and author of *Celebrating Girls: Nurturing and Empowering Our Daughters* and *Understanding Our Daughters, Understanding Ourselves: Staying Connected in the Adolescent Years*

You Can Make a Difference

My daughter was one of those little girls who never seemed to have any questions about her own value and importance. She was headstrong, confident, assertive, always knew what she wanted, and was never shy about letting you know. My image of her as a small child is wonderfully captured in a beautiful photo taken when she was five years old. She is wearing a cornflower blue dress, staring directly into the camera with a beautifully smug smile on her face, and casually holding a plastic machine gun across her body. Even though I struggled with the toy gun issue, I have to admit that photo tells the whole story—she was all right there, nothing held back, and you'd better not get in her way. So what happened seven years later came as a complete shock to me. She was twelve, and she had been acting out of sorts for a couple of weeks, kind of moping around sniffling. When I finally asked her what was going on, she burst into tears and melted down in a puddle of self-doubt, saying she didn't like herself, didn't think she did anything right, that everything she said was stupid, and even her feelings were dumb. I think I must have just stared at her in shocked silence for at least five minutes. I just couldn't comprehend how my tough little amazing wonderkid had so suddenly and so completely lost her moorings.

Over the past ten years or so, parents, educators, and other concerned adults have become increasingly aware that a strong sense of self-esteem in girls is a necessary component to their healthy development in our society. Study after study shows that self-esteem is correlated to success in school and to decreased risky behavior, such as having unprotected sex and taking drugs. And, through books such as *Reviving Ophelia*, we have become acutely acquainted with the crisis of self-esteem that hits many girls around puberty. Indeed, the issue has become so popular that we are in danger of becoming so tangled in jargon that we lose track of the incredibly personal nature of the problem. As soon as we try to talk about it, we are forced to generalize. We start using phrases like "some girls" or "most girls" and "we should" or "we shouldn't," or, even worse, "you should" and "you shouldn't." Before we know it, we have drifted so far from the very real and personal dynamics that set our children up for success or failure that the discussion becomes cold, clinical, and one-dimensional. Even the term *self-esteem* is taking on code-like connotations that invite us to type and judge in record time—as in "She has 'self-esteem' issues."

While much has been written about the problem, there is precious little offered by way of solution, which tends to leave parents and other concerned adults in the dark—we know we want to do something, but we don't know exactly what that might be. This was certainly true for me that night when my previously confident twelve-year-old daughter melted down in front of my eyes. In the eight years since then, I have been reading and thinking about the problem and trying to finding practical solutions.

One of the reasons the books on self-esteem stay theoretical is that self-esteem is much easier to generalize and talk about in theory than it is to approach practically. And while a theoretical understanding is to some degree helpful for understanding the framework we live in, for our daughters, and for all the beautiful girls we are privileged to have in our lives, theory is not enough. Unfortunately, a strong, healthy, and appropriate sense of self-esteem is not something you can produce at will by simply following a set of rules, or guarantee by always remembering to say the right thing at the right time. How could it be, since it is a complex set of beliefs and attitudes that ground us strongly in our own sense of self-worth, of competence, of being loved and loving, of knowing we belong, that our life has purpose, and that we are confident in the unique and valuable gifts we bring to this world?

That being said, it is not true that there is nothing we can do to combat the problem. Healthy self-esteem is the result of being raised, loved, and mentored well. Therefore, everything we do as parents, teachers, and other significant adults in the lives of young girls—how we behave, what we say and how we say it, the quality and character of our interactions, the degree to which we stretch to create learning experiences for them, even the often unconscious attitudes we hold—will positively or negatively impact the shifting core of girls' sense of their own self-esteem.

In creating the framework for our girls' sense of self-esteem, we need to remember that it is ultimately their lives and their task to put the pieces in place for themselves. Our love alone is not enough, being a powerful role model is not enough, the right words are not enough, and our supportive actions are not enough. Our daughters need to *live* the experience of being loved and loving, of being challenged and responding, of taking risks and blossoming. They need to be able to see themselves as competent, confident, and valuable contributors to the whole. We cannot do that for them, but we can create opportunities for their own exploration.

To that end, *200 Ways to Raise a Girl's Self-Esteem* offers a wide variety of suggestions for activities to do at home and school to greatly enhance the possibility that future generations of girls will be bursting with an exuberant, self-confident sense of themselves. Some of the suggestions are about attitudes, others about behaviors. All will have an impact. No matter the age of the girl in your care, it is not too early, or too late, to start.

This book begins, as does everything of value and importance about children, with love. Chapter 2 establishes the foundational and essential role that communicating our love plays in laying the groundwork for all that can follow.

Chapter 3 is also about love, but a kind of love that is too often feared, misconstrued as selfish or simply misunderstood: the love of self that allows us as adults to appropriately and powerfully model for our daughters the kinds of attitudes and behaviors that will open the doors to the world. Regardless of what we say or do in the raising, teaching, and mentoring of our children, it is who we are that counts the most. For it is how we live our lives that our children will always refer to, and that impacts them to the core of their identity.

Chapter 4 is about the power of words: the power to wound, the power to devastate, the power to bolster, and the power to elevate. Language is the symbol of our place in nature. Our ability to articulate abstract concepts places us at the peak of evolution, and that same power is at play in the life and self-concept of every single one of us. We have all at times been both victim and beneficiary of that power. How we are talked to and spoken about, the words people choose to use, all possess the power to expand or contract our sense of self-worth. How much more potent this power is with our children, who have not yet learned how to deflect and discard harmful and inappropriate language!

Chapter 5 goes beyond words to actions, the ways we demonstrate through our actions and our inaction, our attitudes, motivations, passions, sincerity, and commitment to our daughters and the other girls in our care. Often what we do sends a much more powerful message than the words we speak, particularly if our actions are at odds with our words. If we want our children to grow up grounded in their own uniqueness, then we must prove to them by our daily actions that they are indeed deeply loved and extraordinary precious and valuable.

Many theorists argue that it is not self-esteem that is so important to girls, but self efficacy—the belief that you can take action in the world and have an effect. Chapter 6 is an exploration of the ways we can create the circumstances and situations that will provide girls with this experience of self-discovery and the experience of being capable and accomplished individuals. This is an essential and often neglected part of caring for children, precisely because it takes time, energy, thinking, and planning to do it well. But it is extraordinarily important, because as central a role as parents, teachers, and other significant adults play in creating the framework for our girls' sense of self-esteem, it is ultimately the girls' responsibility and task to put the pieces in place.

Chapter 7 is a reality check, a reminder for us to be sincere in our words and actions. Raising children, teaching children, mentoring children can all too easily be turned by task-oriented adults into just another job, and when that happens, we begin to operate on automatic pilot. Then all our efforts can come crashing down in the blink of an eye. We need to remember that, for better and for worse, children by definition have not been fully socialized and, unlike the jaded adults in their life, they can spot a phony or even mildly distracted interaction in a heartbeat. And that is all it takes to turn what was intended as a good effort into a disastrous undermining experience. In every way, at every encounter, we need to try our utmost always to deal with our children with the highest level of integrity possible.

Chapter 8 is a reflection of the many ways we have been blessed by playing such an important role in these young lives, and the awesome responsibility that accompanies that gift. From our socially defined role as caretakers, it is an easy step to begin to think of this as a job, and often a difficult and arduous one at that. So easily we forget, especially in the precious flush of their growing up, what an extraordinary honor it is to be given this opportunity.

I promised you two hundred ways to raise a girl's self-esteem; you will find them here, and more, in practical detail. The constellation of qualities we call self-esteem is perhaps the most important gift we can give our daughters. And what a worthwhile undertaking! There is little in life to compare with being witness to the glorious unfolding of a stunningly beautiful, confident, self-conscious, and self-contained young woman.

Loving: Building the Foundation

Love is at the very core of self-esteem. For children, it is the powerful weave of their parents' love that is the most important assurance of their unique and precious value. When they feel the vibrant strength of that love, they know, even before they are old enough to conceptualize it, and even when they are old enough to pretend to be embarrassed by it, that there must be something truly extraordinary about them to bring forth such a powerful love. Knowing you are loved is knowing you are lovable, and, equally important, it is the necessary foundation for knowing that you too have the power to contribute your own love to the world.

The gift we give our children by loving them fully and unconditionally is the greatest gift anyone can give. So why are so many of us so bad at doing it right? The answer is complicated, but much of it comes back to the fact we were never taught how to do it properly in the first place. It is one of our most glaring tragedies that the vast majority of us were loved deeply by our parents, yet the communication of that most precious gift was often bungled to the point of undermining rather than underpinning our sense of self-esteem.

Out of ignorance, habit, or simply the difficulty of keeping the awesome importance of this task in perspective, it is all too easy to repeat those mistakes with our own children, to love them in our hearts without making absolutely certain they are feeling the fullness of that love. If we fail them here, then we have failed them miserably, for instead of giving them a strong and supportive foundation upon which to build their own sense of purpose and meaning, we will have created a treacherous and jumbled platform and then asked them to do their own repairs.

Do the things that she needs to feel loved.

"The first time my daughter ran from the room screaming 'You don't love me!' at the top of her lungs, I was stunned. I couldn't imagine where that was coming from. Of course I love her—she's my daughter."

Why, after a lifetime of evidence to the contrary, do so many of us simply assume that the depth and breadth of our love for our children is understood and fully received? Of course we love our children—why else do we spend so much time worrying about them and caring for them? But if we are honest, many of the ways we show our love—by worrying about them, feeding them, and providing them with a good home and even great Christmas presents—are not things children experience as proof of our love. These are simply parent jobs—what we're supposed to do. It doesn't mean anything special, and it most certainly doesn't communicate to children that powerful jolt of magic that swells up when love is truly being communicated.

It's not instinctual for a parent to express love in a way that is meaningful to a child, nor is it evident how tremendously important the frequent expression of that love can be. First and foremost, for a child's self-esteem to be nurtured, she must feel constantly loved and know at a cellular level that you love her totally and unconditionally. That means discovering how she experiences love—is it a pat on the shoulder, a look of deep connection, the words "I love you"?

· ·

Parents: Express your love openly: tell your daughter that you love her frequently; discover how she experiences love the most and do that—notes, e-mails, her favorite cookies. Make the expression of love a daily habit. Then listen and watch carefully to make sure your love is getting through. If not, try something else.

Teachers: Teachers cannot make up for the failures of parents, but they can provide a crucial support system by approaching every one of their students with the belief and deep reverence appropriate to their important role in the life of each girl. Find ways to express specifically what you appreciate about each child. Have the children do this with each other; cultivate a learning environment of appreciation.

· ·

Do whatever is necessary, especially when it's hard.

"It's like we speak a different language. Everything I say is either stupid or proof that I don't understand her, and even when I try to get close to her she figuratively or literally pushes me away."

One of the fascinating results that has emerged from the studies about girls and self-esteem is that girls' self-esteem is usually relatively high in early childhood and then plummets at puberty. The usual theory presented to explain this phenomenon revolves around the issues of budding sexuality, body image, and societal pressures, but I am convinced that equally if not more important is the increased difficulty that parents experience in deeply demonstrating and communicating their love for these complex bundles of teenage energy that are our daughters.

When she was an infant, the love just poured out all over the place, in a wondrous unfolding stream of cuddling, holding, feeding, bathing, giggling, tickling, laughing, and kissing. Even as she grew into a child, many of our tried and true methods were still appropriate and used freely. But suddenly, at the moment she's leaving childhood behind, we find ourselves stripped of many of our favorite tools of love—she's too big, both literally and in her own mind, to be picked up and held. Tickling, giggling, and feeding are out; laughing, hugging, and kissing are still possibilities, but suddenly even these must first be negotiated past a minefield of teenage emotions.

For people untrained in the fine of art of making sure our love is heard, felt, and experienced, this is a test indeed, and all too often we fail miserably. We spend more time complaining about messy rooms, household chores undone, and her choice of friends, clothes, and music than we do making sure that our heart connection is sound. At the moment in life when she most needs to be surrounded and supported by our love, we too often withdraw, which only sets off a spiraling series of actions and reactions: she is confused and angry, we withdraw further, she becomes convinced we don't understand her, and so on, until we have inadvertently withdrawn all but the barest shreds of loving support she needs.

Parents: A good rule of thumb, easy to remember but hard to act on, is that the more upset she is, the more important it is that we communicate to her the depth of our love in a way she can understand. Develop some new ways to show your love: make a date just with her, take her to breakfast on Saturday morning or meet her for lunch during the week, and during your date let her take the lead and do as much of the talking as she wants. Just be there and let her know you are there to support her.

Teachers Have the class write a paragraph about how they know their parents love them. Encourage them to explore what makes them feel loved and communicate what they learned from this exercise with their parents and other caregivers. Ask them what is the best way to support them when they're having a hard time.

Stick with It Even If It Seems Unbearable

"I lost my daughter for three years. Even now I can barely get those words out. When my wife and I got divorced, we did a lot of things very poorly, and part of the fallout was that my beautiful, sweet six-year-old decided it was all my fault and she hated me. I can't even begin to describe how hard those years were for me."

Life doesn't always unfold the way we want it to; in fact it rarely does. Occasionally that means our children will be put through a trauma we would much preferred to have spared them from. All children respond differently to serious stress and emotional upheaval. Some get wild, some develop oceans-deep emotional scars, but one variant that is common to many troubled children is that they keep trying, through anger, through withdrawal, by repeated failure, and any other way their ingenious little minds can devise, to prove that they are unlovable. Being the wonderfully egocentric souls that they are, anything bad that happened had to have happened because of them, and they will not rest until they prove it.

Needless to say, this can present us with a challenge of enormous proportions, especially if our own mistakes or decisions played a role in the emotional turmoil they are going through. The world does not come with a safety wrapper, and unfortunately, when bad things happen, it is often the aftermath that proves most destructive, simply because we ourselves aren't trained or prepared to deal with difficult emotional issues.

. . . .

Parents: The most important thing you can do to help a child get through a tough time is to "Hang in there!" It can be exasperating, disappointing, worrisome, and frightening, but be unwavering in your support and stick with it. Spend as much time with her as possible, and don't try to "fix" everything all at once.

Teachers: One of the best things you can do for the troubled girls that come through your classroom is to single them out for special attention, and don't be shy about it. Take a little extra time with them, give them the preferred classroom tasks, allow them the experience of feeling special, and let them know you are always available to talk to. Learn to read the signals that indicate they are having a hard time, and let them know you are someone they can turn to.

. . . .

Nurture the ties that bind.

"There was a time in my life when my career began consuming more and more of my time and my focus. I love what I do, and because of that, it was a very exciting time for me personally. One night I got home early, for a change, and found myself being largely ignored by my daughter. She wasn't trying to make a point, she had just gotten used to me not being around. That experience scared me so badly I let go of two clients the next day."

As a parent or teacher, in case you think you don't matter, consider this. According to *Time* magazine, a survey interviewing 20,000 teenagers "found that kids who have a strong sense of connection to their parents were less likely to be violent or indulge in drugs, alcohol, tobacco, or early sex." According to the same study, "feeling close to teachers is by far the most important school-related predictor of well-being."

On the one hand, this is one of those studies that goes to a lot of trouble to tell us what should be obvious—that love matters, and the stronger the connections and the deeper the feelings that tie us together, the better chance our children have of staying out of trouble and building a strong foundation for their lives. Yet at the same time the study is important if for no other reason than to remind us how vitally important parents and teachers are in children's lives.

Raising children is no easy job, and when combined with all the pressures and stresses of pursuing our own lives and careers, it can, and all too often does, become a nonstop treadmill. When that happens, we tend to see only what is in front of our faces, and focus on only what needs to be done at the moment—finish the report, return those phone calls, drop off the laundry, make a quick stop at the supermarket. Lost in the background is the need to tend and nurture the emotional bonds in our life. No matter how strong those relationships are, they need to be nurtured on a regular basis to keep growing.

· ·

Parents: Make sure your child has your whole attention when you are talking with each other. If you could see a videotape of your encounters over the course of the day, how much of the time would you be focused just on her, free of distractions? How much of the time would you be making eye contact? Touching her lovingly? How much of the time would you be talking about more than practical matters? For a week, pay attention to the quality of your connection. At the end of week, ask yourself how many times during that week did you really feel connected to your daughter, how did it unfold, and what did you feel?

Teachers: In your hectic classroom, how much undivided attention are you able to give each child? When someone approaches your desk to ask a question, does she receive your full attention? For one week, track the quality of your attention to the individuals in your class. At the end of the week, what did you learn? One teacher found that if she put down her paper and really looked at the questioner, she felt much more connection and class went more smoothly. What works for you?

· ·

Create reasonable rules.

"I was so guilty about the breakup that for two years I let my daughter get away with murder. It finally came to a head when a good friend of mine pulled me aside and told me in no uncertain terms I was being a complete jerk and doing nothing but damage to my daughter. It was like lifting a bag off my head. It took three weeks of brutal warfare before my daughter finally believed I would enforce the rules, but every painful minute was worth it."

We don't often think of love, discipline, and self-esteem in the same breath, but in fact they are connected. Self-esteem thrives when you create circumstances where your daughter can stretch, experiment, and take risks without fear. One of the most basic requirements for creating this environment is a good, clear, and consistently enforced set of rules. Some people mistakenly believe that to foster a child's self-esteem, you need to abandon or at least loosen discipline. Some critics of self-esteem-based psychology worry that parents and teachers will fail to set clear limits for children for fear of damaging the children's self-esteem.

In fact, it is precisely the creation of structure and limits that makes children feel loved and safe enough to try out their budding wings. When a sense of order, routine, and fairness permeates their lives, they thrive. That's because they feel safe when they understand the rules you have created and your expectations for them.

In making rules, be firm, neither rigid nor permissive. Create rules that you can live with. (Do you really want to insist that she clean her plate before she leaves the table every night? If not, don't make that one of the rules.) At the same time, don't make empty threats or waffle on discipline. If your daughter knows the rules are only enforced sometimes, she will not take them seriously, and won't behave as you'd like. When you say no, mean no. Don't say no and then give in after she's nagged you. Back it up with clear expectations and consequences you will enforce.

Avoid using violence as a means of discipline. It may get immediate results by stopping the behavior you don't like, but what it does in the long run is let her know in a very hurtful way that you believe she is unable to get the message any other way. Violence also teaches that violence is acceptable as a means of getting what you want. It breeds anger and resentment in children, making them dream of revenge. Studies have shown that abusive parents were themselves abused as children. Stop the cycle of violence and don't model this self-esteem-depleting behavior for children.

· ·

Parents: Encourage cooperation with your children by working with them to establish family rules. When children have a say in the process, they are not only empowered, but they are invested in making it work. Assure their success in living up to these expectations by making the rules clear up front, before there is any need to lower the boom. Be open to suggestions for changing the rules if they are not working. By communicating what you expect while being open to changing what doesn't work, you are setting up conditions for success.

Teachers: Classroom rules should be clear in advance as well. Again, the best rules are the ones that can be jointly developed and agreed upon. An hour spent on this at the beginning of the school year can save a lot of aggravation later. Make sure the boundaries of time and behavior are clear for each activity, as in: "We're going to work on this for thirty minutes, and whispers are OK."

· ·

Get to the bottom of misbehaving.

"My dad was the rule-master. He took pride in being more strict than any of my friends' fathers. My curfew at age sixteen was eight o'clock! Needless to say I became very creative at getting around his rules. The more he tried to tie me down, the wilder I got, until I finally left completely when I was seventeen. He didn't talk to me for four years, but for me it was liberation day."

When a girl starts to act up, we need immediately to pay close attention and try to get to the heart of the matter as quickly as possible, because a chronic discipline problem can quickly turn into a downward spiral that undermines any reservoir of self-esteem.

A sudden spat of misbehaving can be triggered by many things. Behavior like lying and stealing is often a cry for attention. A wildly rebellious preadolescent may be reacting to feeling like she is not empowered and respected within the family. Be brutally honest with yourself before you jump to blaming her. Have you been spending too much time on other things and skimping on time with your daughter? Do you allow her to have a say in developing appropriate rules and boundaries, or are the rules just pronounced? Are you setting enough limits for your girl—or maybe too many? She may be crying out for structure and rules to be enforced; or you may be too controlling and she's rebelling against that. Swallow your anger, put your judgment aside, spend some serious time together, and thoroughly get to the heart of her actions.

Our daughters need to feel that they are important and respected by us; if they don't, they are likely to behave in ways that match their own negative images of themselves. If she believes she is a "bad" child, unable to do things the right way and undeserving of positive attention, then she will fulfill those self-concepts by making them true. The more she is bad, the more she is punished or rejected, the more her bad self-image sets in, and more self-defeating behavior results.

Parents: If, in your eyes, your daughter is misbehaving out of proportion to the normal peaks and valleys of growing up, try thinking of her misbehavior as a failure of self-concept. Think of her not as being swirling trouble, but as having a problem seeing herself as the capable and precious soul that she is. Rather than escalating the punishment, reach out and help her see the ways and places she can succeed. Make an effort to show her that you believe in her and have faith in her ability. Tell her the behavior that you want to see changed, and offer a concrete suggestion that communicates your belief that she can and will take responsibility for her behavior. For example: "You forgot to call me today and I was very worried about you. It scares me when that happens, so please next time keep your promise and check in with me." By being careful to keep your tone of voice loving, yet firm, while still acknowledging that she has her separate feelings, you can show that you have faith in her ability to make changes and succeed.

Teachers: Talk to children who act up. They are much more capable than we often think at explaining what's behind their behavior. Often it's just physical energy that needs to be released, or frustration trying to find an outlet.

Touch lovingly.

"My father died a few years back, but memories of him rise up in me all the time. Lately what I've noticed is how many of those memories involve his touch: his hands touching my face, running his fingers through my hair, his hugs (he was a big hugger), even the way he used to massage my shoulders when he knew I needed his attention."

The power of touch is unfathomable. Think about the things that make you feel special and loved, and chances are that at least half of them involve being touched. Human touch is one of the simplest and easiest ways to communicate love and care. Studies have shown that if infants are not lovingly touched or held, they will waste away and die. Virginia Satir, author and family therapy pioneer, says we all need four hugs a day minimum for survival, eight for maintenance, and sixteen for growth. The best thing about giving hugs is that you're getting them too!

Take every opportunity to touch, hold, and stroke your children and be sure to tell them how much you like their hugs. Your little gestures are declarations of the love they need to thrive; let them know that their kisses goodnight make each day worthwhile. By responding to her with a touch, you tell your girl that you love her for being just who she is; by physically expressing your love for her, you magnify the impact of that love and tenderness, and encourage her to reach out to you.

· ·

Parents: For one day, become aware of how often you simply touch your daughter tenderly. Do you pat her on the back when she's said something sweet? Do you affectionately sweep through her hair with your hand, or stroke her cheek when she's made you smile? At the end of the day, do you feel good about the amount of physical connection you've had?

Teachers: It is one of the great tragedies of modern education that the inappropriate behavior of a handful of teachers has made touching students a dangerous area. Particularly for younger children, the touch of a caring and reassuring teacher can be incredibly important. We can only hope that the inappropriate behavior of the few can be dealt with in such a way that appropriately caring teachers will no longer feel unable to reach out physically to their students. Find ways to provide those reassuring touches that cannot be misconstrued, like a touch on the arm to begin a conversation.

· ·

Foster belonging.

> * *"I was the middle child of five, and it always felt like I was just a place-holder between my older siblings who garnered all the praise and the babies who seemed to attract all the attention. Here I am, thirty years later, and it feels like I'm still trying to find a place that is mine."*

One of the most fundamental ways we demonstrate our love for our children is by giving them a secure context, a sense of belonging in a place that is uniquely theirs. In order for our daughters to be brave little adventurers, to have the courage, the freedom, and the opportunity to strike out in that bold discovery of their own identities, they must have a safe and secure harbor from which to launch and to which they can return. Kids first struggle with finding their identities within their own families, then, as they get older, within peer groups, in classes and clubs, on teams, and in workplaces.

We all seek to feel that we are welcomed and we belong, and yet this is becoming more and more complicated. As family life becomes more varied, with step-parents, significant others, multiple grandparents, step-siblings, both parents working, changing caregivers, and more, it can be hard for a child to feel comfortably settled just as a matter of course. And in school, if a child is shy, or has changed classes, or is a low achiever, the main task in front of her may be to find a sense of belonging before she can really begin to thrive.

Parents: Foster belonging by letting your daughter know the importance of her presence. Telling her very specifically when she returns from a visit to the grandparents how much she was missed and how it just wasn't the same without her there; how much you enjoy her stories, her laughter, her hugs; how coming home and seeing her there makes you smile. Be specific—particularly when there is more than one child in your family, each one should understand her singular importance in your life. What is it about *her* specifically that you cherish?

Teachers: In the classroom, use inclusive language that shows a sense of collective belonging. Start a sentence with *we,* use *us* and *our* to express cohesiveness and an extended group membership to show the child that she belongs to that group. Listen well to the child who appears to be left out; make special time for her to show that she is important, or go out of your way to acknowledge her importance publicly. Listening well, without judgment, is a kind of acceptance, another cue of belonging.

Some kids may feel lost in the large group, so provide opportunities to work in smaller teams as well.

. . . .

Make no comparisons.

"My father's older sister used to tell me I was exactly like my great grandmother. I know she meant it as a compliment, but it always both- ered me. The other day we were visiting relatives and I heard her telling my daughter (who, by the way, is nothing like me) exactly the same thing. I found myself getting angry and then just laughing at the ludi- crousness of it all."

Do your daughter a favor and don't compare her to her siblings, friends, yourself, your aunt Evelyn, or to anyone's concept of "normal." If she likes to wear black nail polish and read Gothic literature, appreciate the strength of her independent thinking. If she spends much of her time ex- perimenting with hair spray, realize that she's showing some creativity. If she spends all her time with her hair tucked under a baseball cap and slapping line drives at the local park, be grateful for her athletic ability.

She's not "just like" anybody, and every time someone says that, she is robbed of a little of her individuality. Above all, be wary of that word *normal*; there is no such thing. Statements like "Why can't you be normal, like all the other kids?" is almost always code for "Why can't you be like I want you to be?" The answer, of course, is that she is who she is, and that is whom we want her to be.

Every girl needs to experiment and explore, and that includes having her fads, fashions, and phases in order to bloom. When a child feels acceptance depends on being like someone else, living up to someone else's expectations, or behaving like someone else's notion of who she is supposed to be, her self-image and sense of her own uniqueness are threatened. It's not our place to try to change who our children are; it is our place to help them discover and celebrate who *they* truly are.

· ·

Parents: No comparisons—even in a loving way. In addition, get in the habit of starting a lot of sentences with "I love the way you. . . ." Whether it's the way she smiles, laughs, tells a story, wiggles into your lap, helps you with dinner, or whatever, just by focusing on the particulars of how much you love the way "she" does it reinforces your appreciation of her own uniqueness.

Teachers: Wherever children congregate, they put enormous pressure on each other to conform. It's one of the more troublesome by-products of growing up. Certainly one of the best things teachers can do to counteract this tendency is to go out of their way to point out and celebrate students' differences—like challenging your class to see how many different ways they can come up with to cheer up a friend. Plan activities that focus on different attributes, such as a "hidden talent" contest, or explore all the different ways one can learn something.

· ·

Ground expectations in reality.

"My older sister got straight A's all through school and a scholarship to college. I could spend forever studying and be lucky to scrape out mostly B's. I know, because for years I gave up most of my social life trying to bring home that one perfect report card. No one ever said I was supposed to follow in my sister's footsteps, but I just couldn't stand the look of disappointment on my Dad's face."

Our girls are born perfect, just as they are. Our work as parents is to make them feel that they are truly beautiful and lovable human beings who grace our lives with all their unique quirks, differences, and surprises. We are blessed to have them, and it is our job, after the discipline, the lessons, the learning, to make sure they never feel that we are disappointed in them.

Admittedly, striking the proper balance between encouraging and challenging them to stretch their abilities and setting them up for failure and disappointment isn't always simple. One helpful thing to remember, however, is to focus on effort instead of results. It isn't our role to *pronounce* the areas our children should excel in, but it is our role to encourage them to put themselves wholly into whatever they do. Growing up is hard enough without getting all the subtle or not so subtle messages about how you aren't measuring up.

At the same time, remember, even if we are very careful, it's still very easy for girls to create their own distorted sense of what their parents and teachers expect from them. We need to keep a sharp eye out for signs that this is taking place, because while the result may appear a good thing (better grades, higher achievement in sports) the lesson is powerfully wrong. We end up training them to lose track of their own agendas, their own needs and desires, in order to please others—not the kind of lessons we want to pass on.

· ·

Parents: Don't set arbitrary goals for your daughter. In school, sports, and hobbies, encourage her to put her best into whatever she does, no matter the results. Look for the places in her life where she really puts her heart into it and praise her to the sky.

Teachers: Much of school is based on grades that reward results, not necessarily effort. To counteract the overemphasis on results, find ways every day to point out and celebrate the hard work of those who aren't at the top of the class but who *are* putting heir hearts into their work—the report, homework, science project, drawing, or school play. As you celebrate the diversity of different kinds of intelligence—physical, emotional, spatial, to name just three—you will be teaching your students respect for these different ways of learning. Encourage kids to set their own reasonable expectations so they can learn that their expectations, not ours, are what is important.

· ·

Honor her choices as much as possible.

"I didn't even realize how much of my own expectations I was loading onto my daughter until she came home from school one day and announced she was quitting the cheerleading squad. My first reaction

was disbelief, and my second reaction was anger. Fortunately that was when I realized something was wrong. After all, what right did I have to be angry? After a little deep breathing we talked about it and what she said made sense. Twenty minutes before I was ready to yell at her about commitment, and now I was just so proud of her."

Each of us is a totally unique individual with needs, strengths, and our own perspective on things. This is, of course, easy to remember about ourselves and sometimes very difficult to remember about our girls. Sometimes we are lulled because we think we know them so well. Sometimes they are doing such a good job of trying to fit into the group of the moment that they seem more predictable than they really are. The moment of truth comes when they step outside of the expected.

Your daughter comes home from school one day and announces that she plans to get her fabulous corkscrew curly hair straightened; that she suddenly hates her softball coach and is quitting the team; that she will not eat spaghetti ever again; that her career goal is to be a professional skydiver—how do you handle it? It is a common impulse for parents to expect their girls to feel like they do on all issues, setting kids up to feel like they risk losing their parents' love if they are different.

If you disagree with her choice, unless you have a very good reason to disagree (concerns about her physical safety, for example), this is the time to bite your tongue and check your impulse to respond negatively to her pronouncements of individuality. For if we can muster the self-discipline to explore instead of try to direct, we just might learn something fascinating about this amazing creature before us. Notice what you are feeling about her ideas, listen to your internal reactions, and then file it away to deal with later.

This is not to suggest that you have to go along with her plans to change her hair, or quit the team, or skydive. But you must show that you respect her ideas and her choices as much as possible. Valuing a girl's ideas has a strong impact on her self-esteem. In valuing your child's opinions and choices, you are showing that you value her deepest self, and that it's OK for her to *be* herself.

· ·

Parents: As much as possible, honor your daughter's choices and opinions. Does it really matter if she wears the blue and pink face paint to the Chinese restaurant? That she thinks Rhonda Fleming (whom you can't stand) is the greatest friend in the world? Draw the line only when you feel it's a matter worth squashing her individuality for: if there are safety concerns, for example, or the feelings of someone else are at stake.

Teachers: Making good choices is a skill that can be taught. Help girls to evaluate and understand their impulses so that they can make better and better decisions for themselves. Role-playing decision making is a good way to show how to explore a hypothetical question and all the options involved.

· ·

Get your priorities straight.

"Sometimes I can't believe I let it happen. I always wanted a big family, but I got so caught up in my ideas about how I was supposed to take care of my children and provide for them that I ended up spending almost their entire childhood working myself to the bone. By the time I realized what was happening I was almost a stranger in my own home."

It's easy to place the blame for problems most kids have today on the lack of time they spend with their parents, mentors, and role models. But the truth is we all have to make very hard choices. Longer work hours mean a fatter paycheck, which may be essential or at least important to fulfill our responsibilities. At the same time, we want to live lives of purpose and passion not only to be true to ourselves, but as models for our children. This is all well and good, but striking the proper balance so that we have real time to spend with our daughters, instead of making up phrases like "quality time" to hide the fact we aren't around as much as we know we should be, is not a simple task. Sadly, just how important this time is often doesn't hit until too late, when our children are already grown.

But something children know instinctively and adults often forget is that the most valuable thing we possess is our time, and how we spend it is a daily statement about our priorities. The way we choose to spend our time sends a powerful message to our daughters about their worth to us, whether we intend it or not.

That message cuts both ways. When we never seem to be able to find the time to spend with our daughters, no amount of explaining and excusing will soften the message that they simply aren't important enough for our time. Conversely, when we carve time out of our busy lives just for them, it is irrefutable proof of just how precious they are. This applies to mentors, caregivers, and teachers as well. Everyone needs to feel that they matter.

Remember, this is a brief window of time that you have been granted, to soak in and enjoy the incredible process of the blossoming of a human soul. Try to keep that in mind at all times, and it will become easier to carve out the time you really need to devote to this wondrous endeavor.

· ·

Parents: Fiercely guard the time you do have with your daughter. Don't just waste time passively sitting in front of the television. Take control over your schedule, and take back the time that just seems to slip away. Insist that the family all have dinner together. Take the phone off the hook during mealtimes and other important family times. Enforce strict rules about television time and computer usage to create more family time.

Teachers: We know that teachers are under enough pressure just to fit the ordained curriculum into the time allotted. But how about "stealing" a little class time for a celebration—a birthday song, a story, anything out of the routine—that will help your class bond with you? Set up a daily or weekly ritual, like sharing time, that allows you to get to know each other more personally. Remember, you are teaching children, not just a curriculum.

· ·

Make time for just the two of you.

"The first time I spent any real time just with my daughter was really an accident. My wife was exhausted from dealing with our newest arrival, so I bundled up our two-year-old daughter and headed out at seven o'clock in the morning just to try to give my wife a little more sack time. We ended up at a local café that provided crayons and an endless supply of placemats to draw on as well as a pretty good breakfast. It was the beginning of a great tradition that still goes on today."

Can you imagine trying to have a relationship with someone who never, ever spent a minute alone with you? At some point you'd have to conclude that, as much fun as you may have had, this other person wasn't really interested in having a relationship with you.

The same is true for our daughters. How are they going to get a sense of how much we love and honor their uniqueness if they never experience it one-on-one? As important as family life is, it is equally important, particularly in families with more than one child, that we carve out time just for the two of us. In so doing, we send a powerful message to our daughter that her essence, all by itself, is worthy of our time and undivided attention. One mother with three daughters takes each of them out alone for a birthday lunch. It's a special time to share reflections on the past year, to talk about dreams of the future, and for the birthday girl to bask in the glow of her mom's undivided attention.

No matter how or when you do it, taking time just for the two of you tells your girl how much she matters to you.

· ·

Parents: Make dates with children individually so just the two of you have special time to yourselves, and try to do it regularly; if possible, try for once a week, but at least once a month. At least half of the time, let her decide what you'll do together. Try a new sport together. Start a Mother/Daughter or Father/Daughter Book Club. Cook a gourmet meal together. Go to a museum. Conjure up a joint project. Find a new trail and go for a hike.

Teachers: Try to schedule some time alone with every child at least each week, preferably every day, even if for a few minutes. Don't neglect the particularly quiet girls. Have the class work on a project independently or in groups while you talk with each child individually. Devise a system where kids can put their name on the chalkboard in a special place to alert you that they want to schedule time with you.

· ·

Celebrate milestones.

"Every year on my birthday my father would end our dinner by standing up and toasting me, and he always began with the words, 'On this day (however many) years ago, my life changed forever for the better.' Then he'd say all these amazing things about how much joy I brought him, how proud I made him and how blessed he felt to be my father. It never failed to reduce me to tears."

Making a special celebration for a child when she reaches an important milestone or learns a new skill is a wonderful way to remind her how amazing she is. Elevating her accomplishments and her milestones to the level of public celebration sends a clear message that, in your world, she is a star.

When her first tooth comes out, when she makes her first communion, when she is baptized or bat mitzvahed, learns how to ride a bike, reads a book, wears a bra, gets an ear pierced, has her first menses, cooks her first meal, learns to swim, tells time, makes the soccer team, hits a home run, graduates from grade school—celebrate!

The possibilities for occasions to celebrate are endless. There is no such thing as too much celebrating. By getting others involved in these celebrations, you multiply how much positive reinforcement she gets, hence multiplying the sense of satisfaction she feels.

The fine art of celebrating is fast becoming a lost art in our rapid-paced world, but it is well worth the attention necessary to bring it back into vogue. When we stop the flow of life to ring the bell and announce a special moment for all to savor, not only do we deepen our awareness and appreciation of life, but we publicly proclaim the place and accomplishments of those we are celebrating. For a girl to be blessed with a celebrated life is a gift indeed, because it provides her with recurring external reminders of her uniqueness and her importance to the group. Celebrate early and celebrate often.

· ·

Parents: Involve your daughter in planning her own celebrations. Encourage her to make the invitations and decide whom to invite. Allow her make as many decisions as possible. When she feels a real part of the celebration, she will be more vested in it, more connected, and it will have a greater effect on boosting her self-esteem.

Teachers: Have classroom celebrations frequently. These can be when a class reaches some milestone like learning how to tell time, or has completed a special project or finished a special book. Every child should be a part of the festivities—making the theme decorations, preparing the food, doing the decorating.

· ·

Surround her with love.

"I sometimes joke that I was raised by committee. My parents had a way of getting every relative and friend within driving distance involved in their lives, and that included raising me. When they had parties I was always allowed to play my part; when guests came over I was never sent packing to do kid things, but was allowed to listen in and even participate in the conversation. From grandparents, uncles, aunts, and friends who have known me all my life, I always had someone to turn to no matter what."

Sometimes it seems we can get terribly proprietary about our children, thinking that only we know how best to love them, when what we need to do is invite as many of the wonderful people we know as possible to participate in this great adventure. It's simple, really—the more fantastic people who get involved in showering her with love and attention, the more unshakably convinced she will be that she is truly something special. Just look at all these wonderful people vying for her time!

Not only does showering her with admirers have a powerful impact on her self-image, it provides her with a wealth of loving resources that will last her entire life. Uncle John may be just the guy she feels she can turn to when she's confused about direction, or her "sort of" Aunt Emily may be the shoulder she needs to cry on someday. With the pace of life speeding up the way it has, many of us have compensated by spending less and less time with friends and relatives and have unwittingly deprived our children of a wealth of loving interactions.

· ·

Parents: Survey your friends and relatives. Are there any who would make good role models for your daughter? How about good support systems? Make the effort to bring these folks closer into your circle. Pay attention to who your daughter responds to, the people that interest her or whom she thinks are "cool," and try to find ways to support those relationships.

Teachers: Bring the world of interesting people from all walks of life into your classroom! You never know what contact will make a difference in a girl's life. Encourage your students to remember and think about people in their lives whom they admire; help them remind themselves of the scope of their support systems.

3 Modeling: Who You Are and What You Do Matter

Mahatma Gandhi said it best: "You must be the change you want to be in the world." His words speak powerfully to parents, teachers, and other concerned adults about healthy self-esteem. In order for our girls to have a strong sense of self, we must have one ourselves—and model it for them.

Because of the way women have been raised in our society, modeling a strong sense of self may be more difficult for women, who may themselves suffer from low self-esteem. But it is essential that you address your own self-esteem issues if you hope to help your daughter grow up with a powerfully grounded identity. You cannot expect your words and encouragement to produce great results if you are a living, breathing example of shredded self-esteem.

This is not an area where you can do for your daughter what you couldn't do for yourself. Just as she will dismiss your lectures on the evils of smoking if she sees you puffing through two packs a day, so anything positive you say will be drowned out by your negative example. After all, if her own mother couldn't stand up for herself, couldn't find the strength or courage to live her life fully and courageously, then how can she possibly imagine that she could succeed?

The same goes for fathers. If we, consciously or unconsciously, behave in ways that demonstrate a lack of respect for a woman's capacity to take charge of her own life, how can we expect our own daughters to overcome the weight of that prejudice? It is one of the great and certainly one of the most difficult gifts of parenting that to do the best by our children, we must first stretch and grow to bring out the best in ourselves.

Take care of yourself.

"When I was growing up I remember making a pledge to myself that I would never be like my mother. In retrospect it was a pretty harsh judgment, but it used to frighten me that she had no life at all outside of being a mom, and I was terrified that I would end up exactly the same."

If you want the girl in your life to grow up strong and fearless, ready to take on her life with confidence and passion, then you must show her that it can be done. Particularly for women, in the ongoing struggle to balance your personal life and your roles as spouse and parent, it is surprisingly easy to sacrifice your own needs until there is little left but the caretaking of others. From afar it might seem a noble undertaking, but the message that gets passed on to our daughters is that it is a good thing to ignore your own needs to serve others.

As you master the art of nourishing your daughter's self-esteem, you will undoubtedly become aware of some of your own unmet needs. Today, far too many women are well-trained caregivers, giving their best to their family and work, yet all too frequently ignoring their own needs. In the process of championing our girls, we feel that it's imperative to do all that we can to foster their sense of self-worth. Yet it is often rare that we do the same for ourselves.

Our children learn by example, particularly from their mothers, who are their primary models of what it is to be a woman. So don't expect your daughter to do for herself what you won't do for yourself. If you want her to take care of herself, feel good about herself, and passionately pursue her interests, she must see you being fully engaged in your own life.

Whether it is regular exercise, reading books, starting your own business, being politically active, treating yourself regularly to some self-nurturing activities, or just carving out time for self-reflection, daily meditation, or journal keeping, by your example, you model the value of self-nurturing for your girl.

· ·

Parents: Take a good look at your life and honestly appraise if you are being a good example for your daughter of a person who takes care of his or her needs. If not, re-solve immediately to take steps to re-inject some of your own passionate interest into your daily life.

Teachers: Let your students in on your interests. Tell them about the great nature hike you took last weekend or the concert you attended. Let them see you as a whole person who pursues her own interests beyond the classroom.

· ·

Do a tune-up on your own self-esteem.

"I was always a very together kid, knew what I wanted and had the confidence to go after it. That carried over into my career where I was respected for my leadership ability. But when I quit working to have a baby, it all came crashing down on me. I suddenly found myself without direction, questioning the stupidest things and just feeling like something precious had been taken away."

Self-esteem isn't something that is once and for all either there or not there. Rather, it's a dynamic and fluctuating condition. One day you feel great about yourself and are ready to take on the world, and another day you just want to crawl back in bed and pull up the covers. But when involved in the raising of young girls, it is essential that we regularly monitor ourselves and do whatever is necessary to maintain our own strong sense of self-worth, because we cannot expect our daughters to learn from us if we are always wobbling all over the place right in front of their eyes.

This means not only paying close attention to our own fluctuating sense of self-worth, but paying equally close attention to the people and things that impact us. Create distance between yourself and any so called "friends" who subtly or not so subtly undermine your self-esteem with half-joking comments like "You look terrible today'" or "Oh come on, you're no good at that." Watch for situations where you are set up to fail, and avoid them—like being pressured to take on some task clearly outside your expertise. Pay attention also to how much of what you are doing is because you want to and how much is because you are easily manipulated by others.

In the press of daily living, it is easy to get so focused on "accomplishing" things that we lose track of why we are doing them. The list of things to do just keeps growing, and in our attempts to be efficient and get as much done as possible, we forget that most of the items on the list are either the necessities for getting on with life, or are being done for someone else. If we are going to hold onto our own sense of place and purpose, we must be diligent about keeping our own interests high on the agenda.

· ·

Parents: Do you have trouble saying no to people and projects because you are overly dependent on other people's good opinion of you? Do you have trouble making decisions on your own without consulting everyone in the neighborhood? If so, perhaps consider taking a course in self-esteem for adults. Or read *The Courage to Be Yourself* by Sue Patton Thoele.

Teachers: Model a can-do attitude in your class. Your competency is being watched and evaluated daily. Read *The Courage to Teach: Explaining the Inner Landscape of a Teacher's Life*, by Parker J. Palmer. It is a wonderful book to help you reconnect with yourself and your love of teaching.

· ·

Revisit your childhood.

"When we found out my first child was going to be a girl, everyone assumed I'd be thrilled. I wasn't. I was scared to death that somehow I'd recreate the painful relationship I had with my own mother."

One of the most surprising gifts that comes from being deeply involved in the nurturing of children is the chance it offers us to revisit our own childhood emotional issues, only this time with the consciousness and compassion of adults. As much as we may appear to children as "all grown-up," we know how bruised and fragmented we really are. Our children offer us this special bonus, this rare opportunity to grow up again, only this time better than before.

As we experience and participate in the unfolding of a young girl's life, our own childhood memories and experiences will resurface, some pleasantly and others perhaps painfully. We have all seen this inevitable childhood return played out poorly and destructively by parents who try to live vicariously through their children, but it is just as powerfully an opportunity to heal old wounds if it is engaged in with awareness.

By nurturing our daughters well, by doing properly the things that were never done right for us, we can heal and smooth over many of the bumps and bruises of our own childhood. Through the love we show for our daughters, we can repair some of that damage to our own self-worth that might still linger from childhood. With self-reflection, conscious choices, and if necessary some good therapy, we can grow with our daughters, and at the same time show them by our example that one is never to old to grow.

. . . .

Parents: The next time you praise your daughter and remember painfully that you never received praise from your father (or whatever your version of insufficient parenting was), send your loving actions back to the little you who so desperately needed that praise. Your conscious loving of the little one still inside you will help her as well as your daughter grow. Remember—we can only give what we have received somewhere— so be sure to give yourself the nurturance you never got before.

Teachers: Conscious teaching is very much like conscious parenting— the more you give to your students the care, attention, and respect you longed for as a child, and send it back to the young you as well, the more you will be able to give from an overflowing sense of self-esteem. Take a trip with yourself to the time in your life when you were the age of your students. What old wounds might you want to heal by being with this age group again? What wisdom did you have then that you want to respect and foster in your students?

· ·

Live fearlessly.

"*When I graduated from college, I went to law school because my father was a lawyer and I didn't know what else to do. I hated it, and I hated it for the fifteen years I was too scared to just quit and do what I really wanted to do. I can't believe the torture I put myself and my family through just because I was too afraid to take a chance. I'm sorry my daughters had to see me so long in a job I hated.*"

Fear is both an essential human emotion and a crippling disease. Without fear, it is highly unlikely we would have made it this far as a species, but in many ways it was a lot simpler back in the days of "fight or flight." In the incredibly complex world we live in today, we are reminded on an almost constant basis that we are not in control. Tragedy unfolds every evening on the nightly news, the media convinces us that we are surrounded by senseless violence. We can see with our own eyes the poverty and suffering in the world. Even purely accidental occurrences can strike at us from nowhere. Planes and automobiles crash, loved ones get sick and die. Hurtful things will happen, and there is no way for us to protect against them.

It is small wonder, then, that so many people, at different times in their lives, become almost paralyzed by fear. However, when that happens, we cease being ourselves. We lose the strength and courage to live our lives the way we want to and our very selves begin to shrink. Ironically ,we begin to inflict upon ourselves the very pain that we are so focused and ineffectively trying to protect ourselves from.

We cannot expect our children to have the courage to face their own fears and the strength of character to rise above them if we cannot lead the way. Fear will always be with us; we fear failing, and sometimes even fear succeeding. We will be afraid that people won't like us or worse, that our loved ones will stop loving us. Fear we cannot avoid, but we can make a concerted effort to keep it from controlling our behavior.

It's OK for our daughters to see us being afraid, if they also see us being willing to move through that fear to embrace that which we truly want in the world. In that way, they'll learn that the way through life is *through*, or as Susan Jeffers says in her bestselling book, "Feel the fear and do it anyway."

. . . .

Parents: Think about the things you always wanted to do but never got around to, the dreams you deferred; take some concrete steps today. Go back to school, get serious about your painting, schedule time for that book you always wanted to write, begin planning for the wilderness trip you always dreamed about. Show by your example that you can always move toward the life you want.

Teachers: Fear is one of those things we don't talk about, so tell a story of how you conquered fear in your own life. Take every opportunity to point out the fearlessness of people in history who accomplished amazing things. Raise the question of what would have been if Martin Luther King, Jr., or Elizabeth Blackwell had given in to their fears.

. . . .

Celebrate your successes.

"I remember being so scared when my first child was born and I stayed scared for a long time. Then one day when the kids were about five and seven, I remember dealing with a few little emergencies while making myself a good cup of tea, and as I sat there at the table drinking my tea and watching the kids bouncing around in the backyard, it suddenly struck me that I was pretty darn good at this."

Raising children is one of the most difficult things anyone can possibly undertake. Not just because it is so time consuming or even because it is so energetically intense. What makes it such a continuously difficult job is that, by the very nature of the undertaking, the rules are never the same. Being a parent is like being on a rapidly moving conveyor belt and trying to keep track of and properly respond to a collection of movies being projected all around you.

When we begin, we are relatively young (mostly), wholly inexperienced, and absorbed in the helpless squirming of our baby. Then, in a frighteningly short period of time we are older and, we hope, wiser and watching our young adult daughter move into her own life. Between those two milestones, the landmarks change daily and sometimes hourly; you must constantly reassess how much reassuring and protection she needs, how much challenge and discipline, how much responsibility she is ready for, how deep a truth she can hear.

At every moment, we must evaluate and try to respond in a way that fits her needs at that moment, that reassures her at the same time it stretches her; that reminds her of the things she needs to be reminded of, while at the same time honoring her for the strength and initiative she has assumed; that opens her to the world in a way that allows her to experience her own power and competence without setting her up to fail. Being a parent requires the wisdom of Solomon, the patience of Job, and the dexterity of a professional juggler, and we will fall short more often than we will ever want to admit.

So when it does work, when you can see, feel, and experience the powerful resonance of a moment well handled, when the connection between you and your children has that almost tangible throb, take the time to relish your success, to appreciate the artistry in that moment, the delicate balancing act that you have pulled off with such elegance.

Not only is it necessary to remind ourselves that we are learning and we can do this well, but doing so presents an image to our children of flawed but still competent and confident adults. And because that image is so true, it gives them the permission to make mistakes and still be proud of their accomplishments. By tracking our successes (and those of our daughters), we construct or repair a healthy sense of self-esteem.

· ·

Parents: Think about your proudest moment as a parent. If it is appropriate (not embarrassing or condescending), share it with your daughter and ask her to tell you her proudest moment as a five-year-old (or whatever age she is now.)

Teachers: Share with your students the teaching moments you treasure as successes. Make a bulletin board of classroom alumni and what they are doing now. Let your students know that teaching is a job where you too are always learning.

· ·

Own up to your mistakes.

"I hate it when I fly off the handle with my kids, especially since that is exactly what my mother used to do with me. But I realized that even if I couldn't always control it, I could always apologize. What used to

hurt me the most with my mother was that she would blow up and
scream at us and then suddenly she'd be sweet as could be and pretend-
ing like nothing happened. It used to make me crazy."

Self-esteem isn't some quality we're born with, or that we have to develop before we're out of preschool or it's too late. Strong self-esteem is like a good bank account that is built up over time, and can always be bolstered. If, like most of us, you've made your share of mistakes with your children, don't panic—just start now to make up for the past. And this applies to your own self-esteem too. Knowing that you may not have done all that you could have for your child is a blow to *your* self-esteem. You can begin to turn that around immediately by acknowledging the times you've made mistakes with your child. It takes a strong sense of self-esteem to admit a mistake; adults with low self-esteem avoid it because they can't stand the sense of inadequacy it creates.

Showing your daughter you have the sensitivity and wisdom to recognize that you were wrong and the strength of self to apologize for it is not only a powerful example, but dramatically illustrates just how important she is. After all, from her perspective, an adult apologizing to a kid is downright earthshaking.

At the same time it is a wonderful object lesson in how people should treat each other. To our children, it often seems like they spend half their time grudgingly apologizing for what really amounts to the everyday excesses of growing up, so to hear a sincere apology from an adult puts the entire exercise on a whole different level. It's no longer just "I did something wrong and had to say I was sorry"; it suddenly becomes clear that everyone should be held to certain standards of behavior and that adults are not the only members of the species who are deserving of respect.

Asking for their help, as in "If I ever make you feel bad like that again, please tell me," reinforces the message that they deserve to be treated respectfully and that they are capable enough to help you do it right. But be sure to back up your promises; nothing undermines a child's confidence quite so much as an erratic and unreliable parent. By modeling the art of apologizing, you are teaching her a real skill. Admitting mistakes takes courage, and she will be profoundly moved by your efforts.

Parents: If you lose your temper, cool down, and then apologize as quickly and sincerely as possible.

Teachers: Good apologies are just as appropriate in the classroom as at home. If you had a bad day and ended up snapping at your class, take the opportunity to apologize to them the next day. If a lesson flops, admit it and ask the class to help you fine-tune it and try again.

· ·

Invite her feelings into your world.

"*I was the emotional lightning rod for my family. If something was wrong, I cried. When things were good, I was the laughing center of attention. Sometimes it was a hard job, but my dad always made it easier by acknowledging what was happening—whatever was going on he'd always say 'Let's check in with Lisa and see how we feel.'*"

In the magical human alchemy of forging a unique personality, what we feel and what we think are the two precious elements we have to work with. In our culture, the thinking part is valued highly, but we do not always know how to deal with the feelings. How many times have you heard someone say something like "You can't feel that way," or worse "You don't feel that way." These are not only extremely controlling and negative things to say, but they are ludicrous. How we feel is not logical, it is in fact completely outside the system of rational thought. It is instead an extraordinary gift that gives us instant and perfectly true feedback and information on a constant basis. Such negating comments are especially problematic for girls, who, in general, for a variety of social and biological reasons are often very much in touch with their emotions.

The truth is the language of feelings is a vital one for all of us. Just as the physical sensations of hot, cold, and pain tell us to put on or take off a sweater or get our hand off the stove, so too, in a much more textually rich way, our emotions are constantly giving us flawless feedback on what we like, what excites us, what we dislike, what we need in our lives, how we want to be in the world. Your daughter's deeply felt expressions—of love, anger, fear, or pain—are all unique expressions of her self, and play a large part in shaping her developing feelings of self-worth. This is information that she needs to have ready access to and be able to understand and interpret if she is going to grow into a strong, self-confident young woman. It is our responsibility as adults to create an atmosphere where feelings are not only welcomed but eagerly sought out. We need to foster an environment where "How are you feeling?" becomes a real inquiry, not just a polite question we don't expect an answer to.

Parents: When your daughter reports in on her day, as pertinent events are related, ask her, "How do you feel about that?" Even if her emotions are disturbing or threatening to you, try very hard to keep your judgments separate, and honor her feelings by respecting that the emotions are hers, real and true.

Teachers: Growing up is largely an emotional experience, and learning how to understand and talk about those feelings is as important a part of our school experience as the core curriculum. Encourage your students to express and explore their feelings by discussing how they feel about a shared event—a playground incident, a movie the class saw—making it clear that we all have our own feelings and that there is never a "right" feeling, only honest feelings.

Wild emotions go deep, girl—you'll be fine!

"*When I was little, I had a really hard time controlling my feelings. My father used to call me 'hurricane.' So it was pretty ironic when I went to see a therapist when my marriage was falling apart only to find out I had overcompensated so well that I had almost completely lost touch with how I was really feeling.*"

Just like in Maurice Sendak's classic children's book, *Where the Wild Things Are*—where Max hollered "I'll eat you up!" to his mother—every child will have negative feelings now and again. The depth of those feelings are not a problem, they are a gift; the problem is we are not always comfortable or well trained to deal with highly charged emotions. Whether she is crying uncontrollably or stomping around in a rage, take a few deep breaths and accept her feelings for what they are. Not only will that help diffuse a lot of the anguish, but it will also allow you to listen well. By giving her both permission and a safe place and manner to try and sort through those unruly feelings, you not only demonstrate to her that you love her and respect her as a unique individual, but you allow her to work through what can otherwise be overwhelming emotions.

This doesn't mean you allow her to act on those angry feelings or just do anything she wants—even Max had to go to bed without his supper. You must allow her the liberty to feel her emotions, but not necessarily the liberty to act on them. If she tells you she hates her little brother and wants him to disappear, don't react to the literal message, learn to read her underlying feelings, and be glad she's expressing her anger verbally. At the same time, be sure to set reasonable limits—physical or verbal abuse from anyone, including yourself, is never acceptable. If things get too heated, calmly and quietly disengage for as long as it takes for everyone's equilibrium to return.

· ·

Parents: Teach her how to kick or throw a ball outside or kick or hit a pillow inside. If she reaches out to strike you or another child, firmly explain to her that she cannot hit other people, and lead her over to one of these safer alternatives. By discovering that strong feelings can be explored in harmless yet very fulfilling ways, and that angry feelings can be transformed into satisfaction and fun, she'll be exhilarated and freed by the new range of emotions that open up.

Teachers: Teach the traffic light method of impulse control. When someone or something makes you mad, Red light: Stop. Identify the feeling and experience it in your body. Then, Yellow light: Consider your options and the consequences of those options: for example, hitting, saying something, ignoring it. Then Green light: Go with the best choice.

· ·

Live deeply, no matter what you do.

"What I remember most about my grandmother was that she had the ca-pacity to make anything seem special. A pitcher of lemonade on a hot summer day took on the power of some kind of magic potion. We would have to hand-pick the lemons, carefully squeeze out the juice and separate all the seeds, and then very slowly add the water and sugar until it reached exactly the right degree of tartness. Then we would fill the pitcher with ice and arrange the glasses on the tray. Then and only then would we sit down and drink."

It's easy to get caught up in the hurried flow of life, but when we do, we run the risk of skimming over the more meaningful moments and oppor-tunities that would allow us to experience our lives in their complete rich-ness and fullness. After all, at the end of our lives, it will not be how much we got done, how many "to do" lists we got through, or how much money we accumulated that will matter. What will be important will be the depth to which we lived our own lives and the extent to which we positively impacted the lives of others.

Begin early by sharing with your daughter the traditions and rituals that you grew up with and then deepen them by tailoring them to what seems to fit your own family. She'll remember these special occasions for the rest of her life. They will become part of your family folklore, the story of your family, and will be recreated by her for her own kids. By feeling part of a long family continuity and taking part in the flow of that continuity, you are giving your daughter a great blessing. To become a part of such a ritualized tradition will give her a feeling of connectedness that will continue to nourish her whole life and will expand her sense of belonging.

Don't forget the food! Preparing meals is such a powerfully symbolic connection. It is how we nurture one another, how we surprise and please, how we survive, how we give the gift of life each and every day. Welcome her into the kitchen, that magical place of love and history. When the special foods are prepared for the celebratory feasts your family may make at Thanksgiving, Passover, or Chinese New Year, inviting her into the kitchen, where women have traditionally held sway for millennia, is to introduce her into a kind of ancient "women's mystery." Involving her in each stage, from the planning, preparing, decorating, cooking, and serving to the feasting itself, you are demonstrating and honoring those tasks that women have always done in families.

· ·

Parents: Create special family rituals. Start with the holidays, since they are usually laden with family history, and expand from there. Hold your own thematic film festivals; start an annual blowout party that your entire family hosts for all your friends; pick a day, an occasion, an idea and turn it into an event to be remembered.

Teachers: Have a discussion in your class about the different ways your students' families celebrate a particular holiday, then come up with a group plan for the class' own celebration that incorporates as many of those ideas as possible. Create traditions in the classroom that help students take their learning and their connections with each other deeper. Choose a class song or write a class poem together that reflects whom you are to each other.

· ·

Teach service.

"One of the things I loved most about the holidays when I was young, was going with my mom to help make and serve Thanksgiving and Christmas dinners at the food bank. It always made me feel like I was doing something important and grown-up."

One of the things that helps firm up a girl's sense of her own worth and importance is the experience of being useful, of being able to see that she can have a positive impact on the lives of others. This, however, is not an experience that is easy to create when girls are very young, because the truth is they are dependent upon others' help. Making sure they are as-signed chores that are necessary and clearly useful to the rest of the household can help, but realistically, most kids, no matter how much you try to get them to see the importance of the work they do, put household chores in the category of "things I have to do because I'm just a kid," in-stead of "my contribution to the household."

One thing you can do however, is demonstrate service in your own behavior, and invite them to participate with you in ways that cannot be so easily brushed off. By showing our girls the kind of positive impact one can have on someone else's life, we open a world of possibilities to them that is otherwise difficult for them to access. Not only do they get to see that there are very simple ways in which anyone can become useful, but we introduce them to a broader concept of how we are all connected and interdependent. It is a powerful experience of context that can only help solidify her confidence in her own role as a growing member of the larger community. Remember, self-esteem is not simply something granted by others; it is earned by working hard and giving to others.

· ·

Parents: Involve your children in community work, preferably in face-to-face interactions. Instead of submitting to the mass consumerism around the winter holidays, do something charitable together as a family. Join a community-sponsored program that gives gifts to the disadvantaged. Have your children pick out gifts, wrap them, and make cards for those kids who have less than them. Show them you have community spirit, and that the time of year is for giving— have them go though their own toys and clothes to give away the things they no longer need. Model neighborly goodwill by decorating and baking cookies and sending them around to your neighbors.

Teachers: Have a class discussion about what students could do as a group to serve their community: spend a morning picking up trash in the park, cleaning graffiti off walls. Have representatives from local community groups come talk to the class about ways they can have an impact. Then decide as a group to take on a project.

· ·

Be clear and flexible in arguments.

"I used to have the worst fights with my daughter until, after one particularly heated battle, I was complaining to a friend who commented that I only had a few more years to worry about it and then she'd be gone. That remark made me see just how quickly she was growing up and that I needed to try a lot harder to understand her and spend a lot less time trying to control her."

Whoever made up the saying that death and taxes are the only two things that are inevitable forgot about kids arguing with their parents. It is as natural as the tides, and it is a great opportunity for us to teach some valuable lessons on conflict resolution. Families who handle their disagreements well—by encouraging differing opinions and welcoming strong emotions; by practicing the arts of tolerance, compromise, reason, and forgiveness; and, most important, by trusting one another to do the right thing—not only negotiate the tough spots together, but polish a strong set of skills that will be an invaluable resource to the girl in our lives.

One of the great benefits of this process is that we both are learning skills we will need. Our daughter is learning how to think clearly, argue logically, and negotiate fearlessly, while we are learning the all-important lesson of how and when to let go and trust our girl's own good sense.

So think of arguing as an art, one that children need to perfect through lots of practice. As the adult, argue well and clearly and be prepared for a wild set of non sequiturs, because most kids, preteens, and teens don't base their opinions on logic. Think of it as debating, a way for them to hone their beliefs and test their opinions. This is all part of the maturing process, heading toward the day when the opinions expressed become more grounded and sound.

In the meantime, don't get hung up on ceremony, and practice the art of forgiveness. Learn how to forgive and then forget. Have an open policy not to go to bed mad, or leave the house mad. Be prepared to compromise and even to give in completely. A good argument is not about winning or losing or who is right or wrong, and certainly it is not about "Do what I say because I'm the adult." It should be a healthy process of airing and sharing views in which both sides listen respectfully and try to arrive at a resolution that makes sense to both parties. Equally important, it is making sure that the resolution is understood even if it is not universally applauded.

A girl who learns the art of conflict resolution become a young woman who can stand up for herself and not be run over by others. The best way to help her acquire these skills is by making sure the people she will argue with the most (that's you) are modeling them for her.

· ·

Parents: Good conflict resolution means setting up a win-win situation as much as possible. In a fight, ask yourself and your daughter, "What is important to you about this?" and see if you can find a solution or set of solutions that honor both your answers to that question.

Teachers: A classroom is a great place to teach conflict resolution. *See Creative Conflict Resolution: More Than 200 Activities for Keeping Peace in the Classroom* by William J. Kreidler.

· ·

Teach that appearance isn't everything.

"My father's family is Hispanic, and it used to really bother me that my grandparents lavished affection on my blond, blue-eyed cousin and pretty much ignored me, the dark-eyed, dark-haired one."

Certainly one of the hot spots when it comes to girls and self-esteem issues is the entire world of beauty, body, fashion, and style. Eventually we all have to negotiate our own ways through that minefield, but an often overlooked step on this trail is the example she gets from her parents and the significant adults in her life, particularly her mother. How we treat our bodies, the often unconscious attitudes we pass onto our children, and the kinds of decisions we make about our clothing, our hair, and the way we present ourselves in the world are all going to have a strong impact on our daughters.

Like it or not, most girls are going to spend some time worrying about how they look, and unfortunately many are going to conclude, after taking stock of all the messages surrounding them, that they hate their own bodies. Our culture has a very deeply rooted fantasy about what the "perfect" female body should look like, and it is a picture that fits very few women. Our own feelings about how a woman or girl "should look" is therefore going to influence our children quite profoundly. If we buy into the cultural stereotypes—even unconsciously—we can do our daughters serious damage.

A recent study showed that black girls are much less "appearance obsessed" than white girls and consequently have higher self-esteem. The researchers concluded that it was because their mothers were more comfortable with the way they looked and less concerned with fitting some "ideal" than white women (perhaps because the ideal itself is one that de facto excludes them).

· ·

Parents: Mothers: Watch your negative self-talk for a week, particularly what you say out loud—"I hate my thighs"; "I've got to lose ten pounds"; "These wrinkles have got to go"—and make a commitment to stop. Fathers: Do you make disparaging comments about your wife's, daughter's, or other girls' or women's appearance? Please stop. Our girls are listening to us, and the more we are obsessed with youthful beauty, the more they will measure themselves accordingly.

Teachers: Break into small groups of five or six boys and girls and have each person tell the group one thing they like about themselves as the rest of the group silently listens with no comments. With younger kids, conclude with talking about how wonderful the positive qualities are. With older kids, have a classwide discussion of what the effect of hearing those positive traits of everyone was, and the impact of advertising on our self-image. Have a story-swapping session with the theme of "You Can't Judge a Book by Its Cover."

· ·

Learn to affirm your own body.

"My mother was seriously overweight, and all I heard growing up was her complaining about her weight and telling me not to end up like that."

It's shocking to find out that today young girls not yet in kindergarten are already beginning to say they don't like their bodies. Yes, our culture does a great job of bombarding us with unrealistic images of female perfection, but for girls this young to get so distorted a view of their own bodies means that very negative examples are being unwittingly perpetrated by the adults in their lives who should be bolstering, not beating down, their children's images of their own worth. Since girls model their behavior after the adults in their lives, working on a more affirming approach to your own appearance can have a profound effect for you both.

Besides monitoring what negative messages you tell yourself (and others) about your appearance, you can start loving your body as it is. Our bodies are the vehicles for our souls, and as such, they are a gift, no matter what they look like. By changing your criticism to appreciation, you model the attitude of healthy self-love that can help the girl in your life stand up to all the negative messages she will be bombarded with.

· ·

Parents: Write down everything negative you think or say about your body for an entire day. Review your list and substitute a more affirming alternative for each negative thought. If you think "I hate my flabby arms" while walking by a mirror during the day, substitute it with a new phrase: "I'm grateful my arms can hug my baby and bench press twenty pounds." And don't limit it to your appearance: "I have a kind and understanding heart," "I am a good friend," "I can jump really high," or "I made a beautiful drawing today" are positive affirmations.

Teachers: Bring in different examples of magazines for your students. Discuss what messages the images, models, and advertisements might be saying to them. Discuss how these various images make them feel about themselves and their appearance. Have your students do their own media inventories, or bring in their own examples of both empowering and demeaning images culled from diverse sources. Start a bulletin board with their examples and written comments.

· ·

Practice kindness.

"I always though my grandmother was the most powerful person in the world, because she had the ability to make every person in every room she ever entered feel comfortable."

When we talk about self-esteem we think immediately of things like strength, empowerment, confidence, having the courage of our convictions. Big powerful words that paint for us a picture of our daughters' having the resources to go out into the world and meet whatever challenges may come. We don't immediately think of kindness, partly because kindness has a softer, sweeter feel to it. It's almost as if kindness is a nice thing, but not something we would think of as powerful. We couldn't be more wrong.

Going out of your way to make other people comfortable and feel good about themselves actually has a double impact on young girls. First, they get to see firsthand, through your example, just how easy it is to be a positive force in the world. In and of itself this can be an invaluable lesson, simply because in the much smaller world they inhabit, young girls can easily find themselves feeling powerless and ineffectual. Just seeing the adults in their lives bringing smiles and satisfaction to others is a constant reminder of the depth of power we all carry with us every day of our lives.

At the same time, it can be a direct benefit when we turn our praise on our daughters. Not only will they directly hear the compliments, but they will be more inclined to take it to heart because it is in character; she realizes "This is the way Dad is," instead of thinking "Oh Dad's just saying that to try to make me feel good." Sincere praise helps build self-esteem because it is an articulated acknowledgment of her value and importance, but our girls are nobody's fools, and if they are the only ones getting the praise it won't take them long to figure out there is something insincere about our efforts.

Practicing kindness is also a way to encourage our girls by example to be positive about other people, and not to be shy about expressing enthusiasm. Not only will they experience the power of positively affecting another person, but it will come back to them manyfold, since everybody loves to be around people who make them feel good about themselves.

. . . .

Parents: In addition to going out of your way to be kind to others, at bedtime, take time with your daughter to review the day. Tell her one kind thing you did and one kindness you received, and ask your daughter to do the same. And be sure to let her know you're thankful for her kindness to you: "I really appreciated your help with the wash today."

Teachers: In the classroom, you can't make kids compliment other kids, but you can model the behavior. You can also ask them to write down a kindness they received and a kindness they did. Read stories from *Random Acts of Kindness, More Random Acts of Kindness, The Practice of Kindness,* and *The Community of Kindness,* and invite students to tell their own stories and talk about how they feel when they are kind and when they are mean or judgmental.

· ·

Create a strong support network.

"There was a group of us who went to college together. We were so close I just knew we would be friends forever, then one by one we got married, had kids, and drifted out of each others' lives. It all happened so gradually I hardly noticed, until one day I really needed my friends and they weren't there."

Good friends are one of our most precious resources. Certainly a young girl with a cadre of real friends has a built-in advantage when it comes to nurturing and sustaining her self-esteem. But it is easy to forget that just as we don't come into this world with a preexisting set of good friends, so we don't necessarily understand the sometimes confusing dance of true friendship. And that is where we adults can have a real impact, by showing through our example how good friends treat each other and how to nurture and maintain those crucial relationships. After all, we are the main social model for our daughter—much of what she will learn about how to make and keep friends will come from our lead.

This means that we must not respond to the increasing time pressures of raising a family by pushing our good friends to the background. Not only does it send a very distorted message of the value of friends, but it also deprives our daughters of the invaluable experience of observing our friendships in action at close range.

Another important lesson that every girl needs to learn is to differentiate between "friends" and real friends. For some people, meeting and attracting "friends" is easy, but getting beyond the surface can be confusing and challenging. There is no easy path through this maze; relationships come in all flavors, including selfish, manipulative, and downright unhealthy. And, when it comes to our daughter's friends, the limits of her tolerance for our "input" will be small.

Far and away the most powerful influence we can exert is by demonstrating as often and intimately as possible the texture and tone of what a real friendship looks like. If she knows your friends, and has experienced the quality of love and respect between you, she will at least have a barometer to gauge her own relationships by.

· ·

Parents: Talk to your daughter about your friendships. Describe what's important to you about each person, and the challenges you may have faced in creating or maintaining friendships. Have there been any friends you have lost? Why? The more she understands the complexity of friendship, the more she will keep her own center in her friendships.

Teachers: Have a group discussion about friendship. What does it mean to be a true friend? The older the kids, the more you can get into issues such as loyalty or thinking for yourself versus going along with the crowd. Have kids make "friendship maps" for one of their parents or older siblings. The person's name goes in the center and the names of friends go in concentric circles depending on the closeness of the friendship. This exercise can initiate great discussion about the qualities of friendship.

· ·

Don't be a hypocrite.

"My father used to go on and on about the 'youth of today' destroying our brains with all those drugs. In fact I usually got the most colorful lectures when I'd come home from a party and he was sitting in his La-Z-Boy with his fifth scotch and soda in his hand. It was such a joke."

It's almost inevitable that girls will experiment to some degree with smoking, drugs, or alcohol, and the extent and the seriousness of that experimentation will be significantly influenced by your own behavior. This is a scary area for parents, because we don't even want to think about our daughters getting caught up in that quagmire, but it doesn't help if we try to avoid thinking or talking about it.

The first and most important issue we must all address is our own relationship to the instruments of addiction: alcohol, drugs (and that includes "prescription" drugs), and tobacco. Like anything else, what we do will have a much more profound effect than what we say—particularly if the two are in conflict. Certainly if we are telling our daughters to avoid alcohol while we are regularly drinking to excess in their presence, both the message and the messenger are discredited. If we try to talk to her about being reasonable and responsible for her health by avoiding cigarettes while smoking two packs a day, our words will become the measure of our own hypocrisy.

At the same time we can overdo the warnings to the point of losing all credibility. Alcohol in moderation plays an important part of our social and cultural tradition. Trying to characterize it as evil incarnate will likely end up convincing our daughters we have gone round the bend, and they'd rather go have a beer with some friends. Lumping all drug use together in one extremely dangerous and evil category can easily backfire. Drugs aren't equally dangerous, and if you skip over that point, someone else will inform her of that fact, and everything you've said can be washed away in a moment. Girls who are well informed in advance about the real effects and consequences of drugs and have strong self-esteem are most effective in resisting the peer pressure involved with using drugs. But it won't help if the information is incorrect, or our behavior is inconsistent.

Smoking is an unmitigated health hazard that any sane person will run from. At the same time, it is deeply embedded in our society. As an ex-smoker (who can freely admit that I love the taste of a good cigarette), I know well how hard it is to reconcile the fact that smoking has no redeeming social value with the millions of people who are completely hooked. If you smoke and care about your children, stop. If you don't smoke, resist being overly harsh in your judgment, but at the same time be open and clear about the truth of any of your addictions.

· ·

Parents: You know if you have a problem, even if you do not particularly want to admit it. Take some time to think seriously about the impact your behavior is having on your children. Talk to your children honestly about your own ragged path through this maze, and about why your current actions are what they are.

Teachers: Role-play with your students the consequences of accepting every offer of drugs, alcohol, and tobacco. What would life be like if we all did this every time we were given the opportunity?

· ·

Give her mentors and role models.

"From the time I was about ten, I realized my mother was a mess. I mean, I loved her and all, but she had very low self-esteem and was extremely negative. So I found myself gravitating to other women for the kind of support I knew I needed—teachers, older girls, the soccer coach, my Aunt Nell. They really helped me see who I could be."

This used to be a lot easier. Until very recently children were not as isolated as they are today. Instead, they grew up surrounded by grandparents, aunts, uncles, friends from the neighborhood. But as we have become more affluent, families have become more isolated. The only adults that children are routinely exposed to are their parents. That both puts inordinate pressure on us as parents and deprives our children of the broad spectrum of resources that they need to blossom.

When we live in small, insular nuclear families, we deprive our daughters of seeing the wide variety of humanity the world is graced with, and their options for *becoming* are narrowed. But when we expose them to a wide variety of adult friends and relatives, they see many options for themselves: Oh, maybe I'll be a deep-sea diver like Uncle Jacques, or the head of a fashion studio like my mom's friend Stephanie. Self-image is created from a wide variety of sources, including role models. By providing her with actual role models (as opposed to images on TV), you are giving her a more accurate picture of adulthood.

Every adult in a girl's life models behavior for her, teaches her in some way how to be in the world. A positive "presence" by any adult boosts a girl's self-esteem, showing her she is important. As the African saying goes, it really does "take a village to raise a child." It's up to you to help find your girl's village!

· ·

Parents: Make sure that your girls are exposed to as many adults as possible. Go out of your way to introduce her to the interesting and unique people that show up in your life. Survey your friends and relatives. Are there any who would make good role models for your daughter? Make the effort to bring these folks closer into your circle. It's OK to ask for their help directly; chances are they'll be honored. A friend of mine just asked another friend to be her daughter's honorary grandmother. She was delighted!

Teachers: Girl also need to be given examples of positive women role models throughout history. Great biographies now abound for all age kids. Assign everyone in your class, male and female, to do a book report on a "Shero" and share what they learned with the class. Invite interesting, courageous women from your own town or city into the classroom.

· ·

Be aware of gender politics.

"When I was a senior in high school I had four colleges competing to offer me an athletic scholarship. I never realized until I took a women's studies class years later that the scholarship that made it possible for me to go to college was the direct result of a whole lot of very hard political organizing and lobbying over a thirty-year period."

Politics is one of those things that you are supposed to avoid in polite company. Judging from the dismal numbers of people who turn out for elections in this country, it would appear that most people's approach to politics is simply to try to ignore it. But when it comes to the underlying issues that frame and determine much of the discussion about girls and self-esteem, politics is an area we cannot ignore. One classic example is Title IX of the Education Amendments Act, which was passed in 1972 after a bitter battle.

Title IX forbids gender discrimination in education activities and has been instrumental is changing the landscape of school-funded athletic activities. Within seven years of its enactment, the number of high school girls actively involved in athletics exploded from around 300,000 to well over two million. The numbers have continued to rise since then. Couple these statistics with the findings that girls involved in organized athletic activities fare considerably better in maintaining and strengthening their self-esteem through the turbulent teens, and you have a powerful argument for being actively aware and involved in the political arena.

The dirty truth about politics is that it is pushed and pulled by a wide variety of interest groups. If those interested in protecting and advancing the rights of their daughters are not vigilant and active, their voice will neither be heard nor attended to, and it will be their daughters who lose.

· ·

Parents: Keep up on the political issues of the day, and particularly those affecting women's rights and gender discrimination. Involve your daughter in discussions about the issues so she begins to understand that what happens in Washington and her state capitol can dramatically impact her life.

Teachers: Incorporate discussions about current issues, particularly gender-related issues, into your civics lessons. Learning how a law is made or about the division of power is much more interesting and compelling if the example used has a direct bearing on your students' future.

· ·

4 Articulating: Using the Power of Words

The old expression "Sticks and stones may break my bones, but words will never hurt me" was a big lie. Words can wound—terminally. By the time we become adults, we have usually long forgotten the extraordinary power of words. We live in a world so crammed full of words that we are only reminded of the impact of words when someone important to us carelessly says something hurtful.

But from the moment of birth on, our children are soaking up messages from the world around them; from their still-new and fresh exposure to the magic of language, the impact and effect of words, especially those from their parents and other caregivers, is profoundly deep.

Children very quickly learn to judge themselves through the words, attitudes, and treatment of others. They develop their self-images through what they are told about themselves, and they learn self-worth from what others say to them or about them in their presence. Self-esteem can be strongly bolstered or torn into tatters simply by the verbal responses they receive to the things that they do. That's why one of the most important things you can do for the girls in your life is to remember that you are a polished and penetrating mirror. Everything you say and do gets reflected back to her, from infancy on, with laserlike intensity.

Babies must be provided with an enjoyable, warm, responsive environment of close bonding, including the innate language of "parentese." From the time she is born, start telling your girl that you love her, and don't ever stop. A toddler depends solely on family and caregivers for the words that will either build or destroy confidence and esteem. A child who is building an understanding of language is also developing a new way of understanding herself. And always, the words spoken to her must match the true feelings of the speaker, just as actions must match attitudes, so that the child will learn to trust what is said to her. Telling a child that she is important and that you love her while you are preoccupied with three other tasks doesn't do that little soul justice.

What we say and how we say it has the power to do good or harm. To love them well, to be an example for them, we must choose and use our words very carefully.

Share your emotions.

"When my daughter was very young I used to tell her lots of stories about when I was a child. What I learned very quickly was that the stories she loved most always involved me screwing up, getting into trouble, or emotionally imploding. Every time we would get around to storytelling, my daughter would scream out, 'Tell the one about how you cried when you didn't get a horse for Christmas!' or 'Tell the one where you threw up on Grandpa's best suit!'"

Growing up is a very emotional process, and our children are frequently caught up in the powerful riptides of these emotions in a way that is difficult and often impossible for them to control. While we can look down from our seasoned perspectives and be very understanding, from the children's point of view, it can appear that they are failing simply because they can't control the flood of feelings.

Children look out at the world and see adults moving relatively effortlessly through life, all things under control, and definitely not buffeted by their emotions. Of course this is very far from a true picture, but we adults often consciously try to shield our daughters from our own emotional issues, and from their vantage point it looks as though adults are always in control.

Our daughters haven't yet learned fully how to manage that roiling white-water adventure of their emotions, and because it appears for all the world like adults don't have this problem, it makes perfect sense for them to conclude there is something wrong with them, that they are in some way inadequate. To counteract this tragic misconception, we need to report in regularly about our own feelings, so our daughters will see that having strong feelings is not a weakness, and that dealing with them appropriately is an ongoing part of life.

In *Emotional Intelligence*, Daniel Goleman revealed the importance of this previously neglected "kind of smart," which has a great deal to do with self-esteem and success in school and in life. One aspect of emotional intelligence is being aware of differing emotions and the ability to label them. When you share your feelings with a girl, you are teaching her not only that strong emotions are OK, but that they can be brought to consciousness, labeled, and dealt with. When we show our children our vulnerable true selves, it is easier for them to accept those parts of themselves and to open up and bare their souls.

· ·

Parents: Share stories from when you were young or from times when your own emotions were passionately engaged so that you reveal your own strong feelings. Not only will you be nurturing a healthy mutual relationship, but you will be modeling for your daughter how to discuss complex emotions.

Teachers: You can practice labeling emotions in the classroom with an exercise Daphne Rose Kingma calls "The Four Winds of Feelings." At any given moment, often below the level of consciousness, four feelings exist in us all—sadness, happiness, anger, and fear. The assignment is to ask yourself, in written form: What am I happy about right now? What am I sad about? What am I afraid of? What am I angry about? It's a powerful exercise no matter what your age.

· ·

Don't impose your feelings on her.

"My mother and father got divorced when I was seven, and they made a complete mess of it, bickering, fighting, and hating each other for years and years. The worst part for me was that both of them suddenly started 'confiding' in me, which was just an excuse for having a place to dump all their anger, bitterness, and confusion."

Being open with your emotions around our children is important, but it is equally important to be very careful about which feelings we expose them to. We want to raise girls who are comfortable in the world of emotions, who have learned the basic skills for navigating through their feelings, and this means raising them in an environment where what we feel is as important and as regular a part of conversation as what we think. However, we can never lose track of the fact that, just as there are subjects that are not appropriate to discuss with children, there are emotions that are inappropriate to expose them to.

Sometimes this is difficult to remember in the moment, particularly when we are going through an extended period of our own difficulties. Certainly most emotional issues between spouses should not be shared with children. Not only are the emotions usually about issues that our children are far too young to understand, but they also put the children in a position of either directly or indirectly "taking sides," and that is something that no child should ever be asked to do. Additionally, serious emotional issues that are more appropriate for the ears of a therapist obviously should not be discussed in anything other than general terms. It is enough to explain that there is a problem and that it is being addressed responsibly.

Part of raising a girl with a healthy sense of self-esteem is making sure that, as the adults, we keep the focus on who she is and what she needs, not what we need from her. Far too many girls are raised to be their parents' therapists and have the burden of coping with adult concerns before their own egos have fully developed.

· ·

Parents: Do you use your daughter as a surrogate spouse, friend, or therapist? Because girls are trained in empathy and are concerned with relationships, they can be easy marks when we are feeling low. Take an honest look at yourself, and if you are using your daughter in this way, find yourself a friend, support group, or therapist to fill that role.

Teachers: Sometimes teachers feel more comfortable in their classrooms with their students than with other adults. Here too it is important to name and articulate your feelings, but in the context of carefully drawn boundaries. Watch for the danger signs when you might be tempted to complain in class about others or about problems in your life.

· ·

Be aware of her fears and anxieties.

*"My grandmother was a wonderful woman, but in order to keep us kids
out of her attic she made up stories about a ghost that lived up there.
For years I was terrified of being alone in her house, and when I stayed
over I insisted on sleeping in her room."*

Why does a five-year-old worry about her parents being seriously injured
or killed? Why is a twelve-year-old suddenly obsessed by her appearance?
Why is a fourteen-year-old refusing to take part in gym class?

Being aware of the fears that children normally have at different devel-
opmental stages can help you cope much better with them yourself, as
well as give you a leg up on helping to dispel those fears. It's natural for
kids at kindergarten age to fear losing their parents, just like it's normal
for sixth graders to be very concerned with how they look, and eighth
graders to be self-conscious about changing clothes in front of others
before gym class. Having fears is natural and healthy, but dealing with
that fear appropriately is a skill girls need to learn. If left to themselves,
their fears can grow and become distorted out of all proportion, consuming time and energy that children should be putting toward learning and

growing, making friends, and building up their own self-esteem.

One of the best ways to help children deal with their fears is to talk to them honestly and quietly. Fear is one of the few things that grows well in the dark, and by shining light on those fears, they can be shrunk down to a manageable size. This is relatively easy to accomplish when our children volunteer their fears, but our society has placed such a deep stigma on fearfulness that children get the message very early on that there is something "bad" or "weak" about being afraid. As a result, often the fears take root and grow in silence, and we need to pay careful attention to the nonverbal cues so that we can expose them to the light of language.

· ·

Parents: Indirect learning is often the best tactic. If you sense that your daughter is afraid of say, big dogs, but isn't articulating that fear, tell her a story about a girl who was afraid of big dogs and how she overcame her fear: "I once knew a girl who lived down the street from us who was afraid of dogs. Then one day. . . ." That way you bring to consciousness and language the problem without her having to own up to it directly. Make it someone you knew earlier in life or when you were a kid, and don't draw comparisons to her. If she wants to, she will. It's remarkably effective (and works on adults too, by the way!).

Teachers: Talk about typical classroom fears, like fear of making an oral report or taking a test, and brainstorm strategies for coping with them. Try to create a supportive environment for listening where stumbles and bumbles are expected, and talk about the things we all can do to help overcome the worst aspects of our fear.

. . . .

Watch your language.

"One of my daughter's favorite books was about a cat that was adopted by the fire department and went on all these adventures riding on the fire truck. For months that book was a regular bedtime request. One day as I was tucking her into bed she told me she wanted to grow up to be a man so she could be a fireman. At first I thought it was one of those cute things kids say, but the more I thought about it the more it bothered me."

There are language lessons and then there are language lessons, and the most powerful language lesson of them all is the words you choose to use around your daughter. The English language is filled with words like *man* and *mankind* that are meant to include women and girls, but don't conjure up equal images in our minds when we hear or read them. Using language consciously and inclusively can show girls very vividly that they are valued and important, included in center of things rather than marginalized.

Because language is so much apart of who we are, changing the way we speak can be awkward. Even when we know that certain words carry gender-biased content, they are still the words we grew up with, and it can feel odd, silly, or even artificial to use different expressions. Just remember—we are raising the next generation of English speakers, and when there are good reasons to update the language, we should be fearless about being the pioneers no matter how awkward it might at first seem.

Instead of using words like *fireman, mailman, businessman, policeman*, and the like, use the inclusive versions of these occupations instead: *fire fighter, mail carrier, business person*, and *police officer*. Whole new worlds of possibilities will open up in your daughter's mind.

· ·

Parents: To increase your awareness of gender bias in the way you speak, when describing characters in children's books, animals during your visit to the zoo, or unknown doctors, construction workers, and members of other traditionally male professions, be aware of how you gender them. Chances are you are saying *he* much more often than *she*. Try to erase gender bias from your speech and vocabulary.

Teachers: In writing assignments, teach kids to alternate the use of *he* and *she* when appropriate, or use the neutral plural *they*. Or arrange a debate on the issue of whether the classics should be rewritten to eliminate sexist language. Make sure your own language gives equal time to each gender.

· ·

Pay attention to her schoolbooks.

"I was forty years old before I knew about Elizabeth Blackwell, the first woman doctor in the United States."

Sexism still exists in school materials. Even with the best of schools, with administration and faculty who are trying to provide a gender-balanced curriculum, we are still far away from being able to take such a curriculum for granted. Many textbooks written from a very male-centric perspective are still in use. Most history is taught from the perspectives of men, and the social sciences, language arts, and other subjects are taught no differently. A steady diet of all the wonderful accomplishments of men, with precious little being said about the important roles and influence of women, can have a devastating cumulative effect unless counteracted.

This is particularly true for fiction; the most revered classics are filled with limiting ideas for girls, and unless these books are taught with sensitivity to this issue, damage can be done. Heroines in need of rescue, women who have to decide between love and career, or no female characters in sight—all of these send negative messages. I'm not against the classics—I'm just advocating that when they are taught, their sexism be pointed out as an historical issue and itself become a topic for discussion.

Fortunately many new books that focus on women's roles throughout history are becoming available, so supplement your daughter's school materials with some choices of your own. Talk to her and explain how and why most of the recorded history of our civilization has been dominated by men and the effect that has had. At the same time let her know how fortunate she is to be living at a time when girls and women are taking back their rightful place as co-creators of our future.

· ·

Parents: Monitor the books that your daughter is bringing home from school and initiate conversations about their biases.

Teachers: A teacher of any subject can affect the self-esteem of all girls in the class and elevate the awareness of their boy peers about women's contributions to the world by spending time teaching through the perspectives of women—women in history, women in science, women writers, women artists—for every subject.

· ·

Make a loving public display.

"I didn't get along very well with my father for many years after leaving home. Every time we talked all I got was criticism. So I was in a state of shocked disbelief when I bumped into one of his good friends one day and he went on and on about all the bragging my father does about me."

Why is it that the best things we say about our children we tend to say to others and in private? We brag about how great she did in the school play, we gush to confidants about how well she is doing in school or sports, and then we go back and correct her English, and nag her about cleaning her room, getting to bed on time, and using proper table manners. We get so focused on our "job" of nudging, correcting, teaching, disciplining, and guiding that we forget to climb to the mountaintop and sing her praises as often and loudly as we can.

Sincere, heartfelt compliments and praise are great confidence boosters, and all the more so when they are publicly proclaimed. Sitting at the dinner table when friends or family are there, and hearing Mom or Dad telling everyone what a fabulous job she did on her science project or how she pulled off a major-league slide going into third base can be a powerful and deeply engraved event. Children know intuitively that as the number of people present at a gathering increases, the relative importance of any one person there decreases. Therefore when a child is singled out and raised up to the crowd for approval, it can go a long way toward convincing them that they are indeed incredibly and uniquely special.

Of course, like anything else, this can be overdone. If you constantly point out her achievements to one and all, she may get the sense that she is only valued for what she can do, for her ability to give you "bragging rights" among parents. And don't forget to honor her privacy as well. Chances are she doesn't want to hear it proclaimed publicly that boys are now calling or that she got her first period. Be sensitive to the content as well as the context of your praise!

· ·

Parents: When was the last time your daughter heard you tell someone how fabulous she is? If it's been a while, how about finding the next opportunity? When you do so, be specific—kids want to hear why you are impressed, not a blanket "She's great."

Teachers: This can be tricky in classrooms, because kids don't want to be singled out as the teacher's pet, but as long as you spread the praise out to everyone over time, there should be fewer problems. But make sure to include the quiet ones, the less stellar students as well—"Good job on the decorations, Fred"; "Way to hit the ball, Juanita."

· ·

You look marvelous, darling.

"I think the words I head most from my mother for the last four years I lived at home were 'You're not going to wear that, are you?'"

We are a culture obsessed with appearances. The more you look at it, the funnier it gets—except it's so damaging. Each fashion season, beauty gets redefined again (although rail-thinness has been holding damaging court for decades now), and inevitably the "norm" is something that is unattainable for at least 90 percent of us. Then we pour millions of dollars into advertising and television programming trying to convince ourselves that there is something real about all these silly images. What is real, however, behind the one-dimensional cultural icons, is that true beauty has nothing to do with clothes, hairstyle, or cheekbones; it has to do with the strength and resonance of a person's heart and soul, and *that*, as a society, we pay precious little attention to.

While we cannot completely inoculate our girls from these cultural forces, we can offer a different perspective. We can compliment her sturdy legs for allowing her to finish the race, kick the soccer goal, dance to the latest CD; her strong arms for throwing the fastest curveball and giving us the best hugs. We can also make sure to point out when her soul shines through while she is doing something—telling us a story about her day, patiently picking up her little brother for the forty-seventh time that day, humming quietly to herself—that she is beautiful.

In some ways we are at the darkest moment in history for women and their body images, because while the advertising industry has polished its craft and perfected its broad-spectrum assault on the minds and beliefs of young women, we as a society have just begun to understand its incredibly damaging and insidious effect. But the tide is turning: recently, the

National Organization of Women launched a major campaign to force advertisers to adopt a code of ethics that would forbid the kinds of advertising that use women's body parts to sell products. We need to take control of the image-making machinery and begin showing the kinds of true beauty that come from the depths, from the heart, from the soul.

· ·

Parents: When your daughter comes bounding into the house in the full flush of excitement over something she is engaged in—a school project, a ball game, the new friend she just made—tell her how exquisitely beautiful she looks! Let her know how much she lights up the world when she laughs, how her smile sparkles, and how, when her essence shines through, there is nothing in any fashion magazine that can match her.

Teachers: It's important to acknowledge the effect of passionate interest in the classroom as well. As you get to know your students you can anticipate when they might "shine" in a particular activity. Don't hesitate to tell a girl how vibrant she looks when doing the science project or how alive she feels to you when she is drawing.

· ·

Give her roots.

"One of the things I loved most about visiting my grandparents was camping out in front of my grandfather's chair every night after dinner and listening to him weaving these fabulous stories about the Old Country, about the long hard journey to America, and all the wonderful but difficult times they went through."

Much of your daughter's sense of identity will come from you, and much of that depends on how good a job you do in giving her a strong foundation of family and ethnic pride. Much of that pride will come directly from the stories you tell.

We are a storytelling species. In a very important way, this is the crucial difference that separates us from the rest of the animal kingdom—we can remember, distill, and pass on information to the next generation, and the way we do it is through stories. Give your daughter a richly textured picture of where she comes from—both personally and as part of an ethnic group. Connect her with your words to the places and people that preceded her. Help her to see the ways that her heritage, her family history, and her cultural background have and can impact her life.

When we give our daughter this kind of historical context, she will have a sense of roots, a sense that something solid, an irrefutable and indestructible beginning, is holding her up. This is important in the diverse society we live in, where so many kids feel "less than," "ugly," or otherwise unacceptable because they do not fit the stereotype of the white middle class. Family and ethnic pride helps counteract those forces that demand our girls all look like they came from the same cookie cutter. Such an exposure will also help her appreciate the ethnic roots of her friends and classmates, and help break the destructive cycle of racism and self-hatred.

So tell her stories about her grandparents, her great-great-uncle, your own childhood; intersperse those with stories about what she was like when she was a baby. Realize that she listens intently to what you say, whether she shows you this or not, so invest your stories with as much pride and texture as you can. Not only will she love to hear these stories, but they will also help strengthen her sense of security and confidence in her own ability to forge connections in the world. She'll learn about the continuity of things, and she'll see her own future as part of that long line.

· ·

Parents: Read books or see documentaries together that illuminate a time in history that was relevant to her family's history. Did her forebears come here as a result of famine? The Holocaust? The slave trade? Help her understand the context into which she was born. She will make associations that she will build on and gather strength from throughout her life.

Teachers: Assign students the task of interviewing their parents or grandparents about their ancestors. Ask them to find out what countries their parents or grandparents or great-grandparents were from, or what states. Using a map of the world, have the children pin slips of paper with their names on them to the countries that members of their family have come from. Have them do all four grandparents, or any number of relatives.

· ·

Teach her the secret of advertising.

"I was fifteen years old, working for a dollar-seventy an hour at a greasy fast-food restaurant and I had to, I mean had *to, have a fifty-dollar pair of designer jeans. Was that crazy or what?"*

How many times have we all witnessed the screaming battle at the toy store where some poor kid (who has, no doubt, before the age of five logged thousands of hours of television), is throwing a fit because he must, *must*, have the latest action figure. It's not a pretty picture, and in that context we can see clearly the absurd effects of advertising. What is much more difficult to see and what we usually neglect to address is how pervasive this socially induced behavior manipulation is in our society. That is dangerous, because until our daughters understand that they are targets, they will be understandably susceptible to the siren call of advertising and fashion that will only lead them away from their true selves and into an expensive (that's the whole idea, after all), frustrating, and unhealthy pursuit of image over substance.

They need to know the truth and they need to hear it from us. They need to know that rooms full of very well-paid executives daily plot ways to fool them into believing they must have this face cream or that pair of jeans or those shoes, because they are somehow inadequate without these things. Regularly remind them that the goal of the media is to make money off you and your girls, their target market, and their sole motive is profit. Unless our daughters understand this at a deep level, they will always be at the mercy of the image-makers who routinely undermine self-esteem in order to sell products.

By regularly and relentlessly exposing this billion-dollar charade, we can give our daughters the information they need to make intelligent decisions, help them inoculate themselves from the hypnotic lure of glitzy advertising, and, most important, remind them that it is not what other people say or think that is important—what is important is what they feel and what they think for themselves. Helping them resist the social pressures to be "just like. . ." can only build a stronger sense of self.

· ·

Parents: Suggest to your daughter that you do a one-day "study" to try and discover what the media is pushing today. Spend an afternoon looking over your favorite magazines, or take one night to watch television. With older kids, have them write down their observations about what messages are being communicated by the ads. Take turns making observations, being careful not to judge each other's responses. With younger kids, watch one ad on TV together or look at one toy ad in the newspaper. What are the advertisers trying to sell? What are they saying about her?

Teachers: Have your class talk about times the media has influenced them. Then be honest and share a story about how you have changed your appearance, or "had to have" something through the influence of the media. Simply discussing these observations and influences will help foster understanding.

· ·

Accentuate the positive.

"A teacher friend of mine recently turned me onto the idea of 'asset focus,' that kids learn best when what they do right is pointed out, rather than what they do wrong. It really made an impression on me, and I decided to try it for myself. So far, it's really working!"

When so much of raising a child is about teaching and challenging and setting boundaries, it is easy to get stuck in a mode of constant criticism. We notice all the mistakes, all the things not done that should have been done, all the irritating sloppy little "habits" our darlings have developed, and we almost can't stop ourselves from nagging, complaining, correcting, demanding, and snapping. It's a rare parent or teacher who never loses patience with the children under his or her wing. Most of us, try as we might, find ourselves short-tempered more often than we care to admit. If you feel your patience thinning out by the day, and find that everything coming out of your mouth is negative, stop! It isn't going to help them, and it sure doesn't feel good to be reduced to a constant complainer.

The truth is, the human brain is actually wired to track what works and to discard all else. (Think of a baby learning to walk—she doesn't yell at herself for falling down. She notes what worked in the attempt and tries again.) Other scientists label it "positive reinforcement." Whatever we call it, the more we can focus on what our daughters are doing right, the more we go with the natural patterns of the mind, and the more we help her notice what's right about herself as well. Which, besides being an esteem booster, will go a long way toward her adopting positive behaviors and dropping negative ones.

· ·

Parents: For one day, ignore all the things your daughter does that you can't stand. Catch her doing things right instead. Ignore that she arose late, ignore the uneaten food, the unrecognizable table manners, the ripped shirt, the ugly nail polish—ignore everything that would ordinarily provoke you. When you feel a negative remark rising in your throat, count to ten, or count to twenty, and hold your tongue. Notice the positive things instead. Keep this positive behavior up all day, and you'll definitely notice a change. If your children become suspect, and say, "Where did my real dad go, the one who notices everything that I do wrong?" you'll know you are making progress.

Teachers: For a month, grade papers by marking all the correct answers rather than the wrong ones. Notice if it has any effect on your students' performance. Comment on the kids behaving well rather than pointing out the misbehavers. Eliminate *Don't* from your vocabulary. Turn "Don't forget your field trip money," into "Remember to bring your field trip money."

· ·

Talk about sex.

"From the time I was little, at least twice a year my dad would have the 'sex' talk with me. His speech was basically about how wonderful it was but that it was also really powerful and not something to be played with or entered into before you were really ready. At the time it was always awkward and embarrassing, and I remember mostly just trying to get it over with or saying 'Yeah, I know, Dad' a lot, but secretly it always made me feel better."

OK, so this is really hard to do because you just know you're going to get embarrassed, and your daughter's reaction, at least as she gets older, is going to range from general discomfort to mortification, but it is crucially important to talk to her about sex.

The reasons are pretty basic. If you don't talk about it, you just create a forbidden zone which any self-respecting young girl will be attracted to like a moth to a flame; second, if you don't, then you abdicate her sex education to her friends, and there you face the dueling dangers of her getting incorrect information (when I was in college in the '70s a friend of mine at an Ivy League college actually thought you wore a diaphragm around your neck to prevent pregnancy), or good information but without the framework of the values you might prefer. Also, if you avoid this topic, you are sending her the message that you don't think she is mature or sensible enough to discuss sex. Finally, if you think not talking about sex is somehow going to make it go away, think again, and remember, at this point in time we are not just talking about sex, we are talking about life and death.

A recent study done with sexually active teenage girls and their mothers found that girls who had discussed safe sex with their mothers were three times more likely to use a condom than girls who had not had that discussion. So start early and repeat yourself with some regularity.

· ·

Parents: When was the last time you talked about sex with your daughter? It's easy to let this slip away in the press of daily life. The best discussions come up in context— a friend of yours is pregnant, your daughter is confused by newspaper headlines. But if you think back and realize that such circumstances don't arise regularly enough, mark your calendar and do it. Read a good book or get a book for your daughter and you to read together. (No putting it on her bed to discover on her own, as many parents of our generation did—you have to indicate a willingness and ability to talk about this.)

Teachers: Teachers' hands are tied on this issue, in many cases, by school boards, but if there is "wiggle room," be sure to take it. And when policy is being set, let your voice be heard—remember, when it comes to girls and sex, information can be lifesaving.

· ·

Know when to be silent.

"I played a lot of volleyball in school, and I used to hate it when I had a real lousy game and then had to listen to my father trying to be the good reassuring dad, telling me how great I was."

Our daughters need to hear our words. They need to hear the delight in our voices when we are with them, they need to hear the pride and satisfaction when we talk about their accomplishments, they need to hear the love, tenderness, and joy they bring out in us expressed in words. They need our empathy when they are hurting.

But at the same time, our words must be sincere, consistent, and carefully used; they must ring with truth in order to be effective. And we need to remember that sometimes silence is golden.

If we hand out praise carelessly, we diminish its worth, and she will be the first to know. If we congratulate her on a job well done when she feels strongly that her effort was less than wonderful, we not only are ineffective in our attempt to make her feel better about herself, but do long-term damage by undermining our own credibility. If we gush on and on about something she feels is no big deal, we may undermine our daughter's sense of self-esteem by inferring we don't think she is able to handle the hurt herself.

Words are powerful, and it is tempting, in our desire to strengthen our daughter's self-esteem, to lean heavily on the power of words to bolster and cement her sense of worth, importance, and competence. But we need to be very aware of the delicate balance between clearly articulating our love and pleasure in her, and sliding overboard into the dangerous territory where our words begin to have the opposite effect and not only undermine her self-esteem, but reduce us to bystanders whose words cannot be trusted.

· ·

Parents: Instead of being left out in the dark about what she might want, trying to intuit what's needed, teach your daughter to ask for what she needs by surveying her own inner emotional landscape and then reporting back to you: "I'm sad because I got a B on the test. I need a little praise now," "I feel lonely. I need a hug." You can do this by modeling it yourself and by asking her when she is upset what she might need from you. It's a powerful way to build self-awareness and the confidence it takes to ask for what we need from others!

Teachers: Overdone praise is just as ineffective in the classroom as at home. Make sure your compliments are genuine, or don't say anything at all. Kids know when they've let themselves down on an assignment. Ask how they would do things differently.

· ·

Avoid sarcasm and teasing.

My father and brother teased me all the time growing up. It made me feel horrible about myself—both what they said and the fact that I couldn't take it as a joke."

Ah, teasing. I am an inveterate teaser. It's a way for me to show in an indirect way my feelings of love and connection to the person I'm teasing. But I have learned over the years from the girls and women in my life that it is rarely received in the spirit in which it was offered. Perhaps it is a gender issue; in my experience, many more men are comfortable with teasing and sarcasm than women. Over and over, women tell me of the terrible wounds to their self-esteem they have suffered as young girls from the teasing of, most usually, their father and brothers. One woman I know goes so far as to claim that all teasing is a hostile act.

The problem with teasing, as I've come to see, is that the words meant in jest have nonetheless been spoken and, in some almost alchemical way, become real even if they are meant to be harmless. A statement like, "You don't know anything about that, now do you?" is either a tease or a truth depending on tone of voice. But the words themselves are wounding and often the tone is irrelevant to the listener. Also, because so many people have learned to hide their truth in teasing, often teasers actually do mean what they say, and therefore their words are intentionally hurtful.

Because teasing and sarcasm can so easily be misconstrued, if we are concerned with bolstering the self-esteem of the girls in our care, it's probably best to avoid these modes altogether. If you find that difficult (as

I do), at least be sensitive to the areas where girls should never be teased—their looks (too loaded in this culture) and their competency (it's far too easy to reinforce insecurity). If it appears that you have hurt a girl by your teasing, be sure to apologize, and if she asks you to stop, respect that boundary, rather than teasing that she lacks a sense of humor.

· ·

Parents: Do you have a tendency to tease? Often these patterns have been set in our own childhoods, and we may be oblivious to them. Warning signs: You've been asked by other people to stop teasing, or others have been offended by things you said in jest. Chances are you're hurting your daughter's feelings too, even if she has said nothing.

Teachers: Break into small groups to discuss teasing. How does it feel to do it? To be on the receiving end? Is it ever OK? Is there nothing taboo? Have one student in each group summarize the group's conversation to the class as a whole. When age appropriate, do a lesson on sarcasm. Many children don't always recognize it or understand it when they hear it; some just know there is something wrong with what was said that doesn't feel right. Understanding sarcasm and it's impact is an important tool for self-defense.

· ·

5 Showing: Demonstrating Respect for Her

We can love them, we can lead by example, we can use the power of our words to bolster their confidence and encourage their efforts, but we must also show our daughters through our day-to-day actions that our love is not removed and our words are not hollow. Each day they are in our care, the actions we take or do not take demonstrate to the girls in our lives that we have respect for them—or that we don't. Through careless actions, through putting down her choices of friends, of wardrobe, of book reports, or whatever, we send a strong message that we don't trust her to make wise choices, and that we don't respect the choices she makes. This does immeasurable damage to self-esteem.

Our job as caretakers is to help our daughters learn to make good choices, and to affirm our belief in their ability to make wise choices. We do that, in part, by respecting as much as possible the choices they do make, and by demonstrating our deep respect for who they are as human beings. We show her through our patience and our willingness to tackle difficult issues such as sexual harassment and abuse, which are violations of respect. We show her by listening deeply to what she has to say even when it is not necessarily clearly articulated. We show her by trying mightily to understand the world as she experiences it even though we will always come up short. We show her by being willing to bend our schedules to make her the priority in the day-to-day unfolding of life. And we show her by walking the incredibly fine line between providing the safety and security she needs to become fearless, and challenging her to stretch, grow, and think for herself as often as possible.

Watch your body language.

"She frequently calls her daughter pet names, like 'little princess.' But what sounds like a tender compliment seems more like a belittling name when you hear and see how she says it—her body language, the context, and the tone of her voice, with arms crossed, nose wrinkled, and brow furrowed as she speaks. Her daughter shrinks with humiliation and knows her mother sees her as ungrateful and impossible."

Other than words, the way we communicate most often is through body language. Our words may hold meaning, but the way our body complements or contradicts those words shows our true feelings. Through the way we are sitting, the way we gaze, our gestures, through every combination of physical poses possible, we shed light on our true feelings, and our children are masters at interpreting every nuance that is being communicated.

Remember, from the time they were born they have been studying us with an unbelievable intensity; knowing our moods and our feelings is a central part of their job. Add to this the fact that during the crucial formative years before they began to master language, their focus has been on how we communicate nonverbally, and it is easy to see how much information children pick up from even the most subtle shrugs, signs, or facial expressions. Like it or not, we are an open book to them.

So when we respond to their report of the day's activities by rotely saying "That's wonderful" without taking our eyes off the newspaper we are reading, the message we're sending isn't wonderful at all, it is terribly deflating. She knows that in that instant, reading the newspaper was more important to you than listening to her.

These are not subtle messages; they can be very damaging to her sense of self-importance and confidence, and unfortunately we can and very often do deliver them innocently and without even knowing we are doing it. After all, we're busy—how are we going to make dinner, catch up on the news, and pay attention to our daughter's concerns if we don't "multitask"?

Beyond that problem lies a more subtle one—our words and our body language must match up. If we say, "You're doing a great job," you have to mean it—with your smile, your encouraging eye contact, your hand on her shoulder. If you say one thing and demonstrate another with your body language, your daughter will pick up on the hypocrisy.

· ·

Parents: If you live with another adult, have your partner point out (privately!) when your words to your daughter and your body language conflict. If you live alone with your child, ask a friend to notice when you are together. Often other people can see things that we are not aware of.

Teachers: When I was in school, I could always tell which kids the teachers liked and which they didn't; it was just something in the way they related to the students that was obvious. While you can't completely control your natural preferences, you can be sure to give every child as warm a smile as possible, and be aware that the kids in your care know exactly how you feel. It may help to think of each child as a soul who is struggling to find her way, even if that way is unpleasant to you.

· ·

Watch for unconscious bias.

"My mother, grandmothers, and aunts will deny this, but they have al-ways preferred my brother to me simply because, I believe, he is male. They make a big fuss over everything he says and does, while I am left there, a second-class citizen."

Because we have all been raised in a society that favors males over fe-males, none of us is completely free of gender bias. The most we can do is become as conscious of it as possible and to do all we can to make the girls in our care feel as valued as possible. Because of the way they were raised, older generations probably have this prejudice more than younger ones, and a visit to Grandma or Great-grandma can be an occasion to dis-cuss sexism with your daughter.

Whatever you do, if you are witness to a blatant put-down of girls in general, or to your daughter because of her gender, or even a subtle ignoring, don't let it go past unnoticed. You don't have to attack the offender, but you should always raise the issue later with your daughter: "I bet that felt bad when Grandpa said . . . I'm afraid he doesn't know any better when it comes to things like that." If it's appropriate, you can also privately say something to the offender, "You know, Molly, it makes Tiffany feel unimportant when you focus so much attention on Tim and don't even ask her anything about her life."

When we make note of it, we let our girl know that we disapprove, and we give her an opportunity to become more aware and articulate about the problem. We also give her a chance to repair her damaged self-esteem by placing the problem squarely on the other person, not on herself.

If you think we've all progressed past this issue, think again. A teacher trainer friend of mine recently went into elementary school classrooms to count how many interactions teachers (mostly female) had with male students and how many they had with females. You guessed it—the boys are still getting a disproportionate share of the attention. And recently a middle-school class came to my office for a "Take Kids to Work Day." My coworkers commented on the vast gender gap—the boys were raising the hands to ask questions; the girls were hanging back silently, reticent to speak even when called on directly.

· ·

Parents: Take an moment to do an honest assessment of your own behavior. Do you pay more attention to your son? Does he get more airtime at the dinner table? Awareness precedes change.

Teachers: Make a list to post on your desk with two columns: boys and girls. Then, for a week, go about your normal day. Every time you have an interaction with a child, note their gender. At the end of the week, count up each column. Is the split proportionate to the class demographics? If not, you can make a conscious decision to call on as many girls as boys. Continue to keep the list and see if it changes.

· ·

Listen well.

"My dad worked out of an office behind our house, so we had ready access to him when I was growing up. What I remember most strongly to this day is how well he handled our constant interruptions. He always greeted us with a big smile and his full attention. It made me feel particularly special to know that I could always talk to him, even when he was in the middle of important work."

Good listening skills are one of the most important prerequisites to caring for children. When they are infants, we need to hone our ears to be able to decipher the cranky cry from the wet cry from the scared cry. As they grow, we need to learn how to hear the meaning behind their words. As they struggle with both the depth and difficulty of language and the much more complicated job of trying to translate what they feel into words that adequately convey their meaning, we need to be their receptive interpreters.

Children who are listened to learn to speak earlier and are more socially outgoing and confident as the years go by. Yet at times it's hard to keep it all in perspective, simply because children have such an extraordinary capacity to go on and on. Of course our energy will wane, and we will find it difficult to be 100 percent attentive all the time, but we need to give it our best effort.

She's chattering on about the robot she made today in preschool, or the new girl on the bus—those things are very important in her world. When we do our best to answer her barrage of questions, we reinforce her sense of self-worth. If we listen well, she will know that her opinions and feelings are being taken seriously, and hence she will feel valued.

Young children often don't know how to talk about their feelings, so part of "listening" to young kids is helping them put what they feel or think into words. So be attentive, look for clues from body language, be sensitive to what she may be leaving out. Children whose age is in the double digits (ten and older) should be pretty articulate about what they are feeling. It is important to let kids this age and older have the time to talk out their ideas and problems. Try not to interrupt, put words into their mouths, or talk too much. To show you are listening, stay in the conversation by occasionally recapping a conclusion your child has made, using different words.

· ·

Parents: Part of what we're trying to impart when we talk about self-esteem is what social scientists call an "internal locus of control." What this means is that a person with strong self-esteem can make her own decisions and not be swayed by "the crowd" because she has learned to be the barometer of what is important to her. We can reinforce this in our listening by asking the question, "What is important to you about this?" when she voices a strong feeling or opinion. In that way, she'll learn to count on her own opinions, feelings, and values, not on anyone else's.

Teachers: One way to show respect for what your students have to say is to be very clear with them about when you can give them your full attention and when you can't. If you are in the middle of things, tell them what they have to say is important enough to you that you want to set a time when you can give them your full attention—then make sure you follow through.

. . . .

Practice seeing the world through her eyes.

"I don't know how she did it, but my mom had an incredible knack for coming through when I really needed her. We had our share of fights and we'd go weeks when I felt like she was on my case about every tiny thing, but then—bam! Something would really upset me, even things that happened at school she couldn't have known about, and out of the blue she'd be there saying and doing just the right things to make me feel better."

The one thing we all want more than anything else is to be understood for who we really are. Such a simple thing, and yet seemingly so incredibly elusive. One of the great opportunities that we are given as parents is to provide exactly that to our children—understanding. And it is precisely in the employment of this magic that we can have our most powerful effect on our daughters. The irony is that understanding them can be difficult.

For most of us this has come as somewhat of a surprise. For some reason we seemed to assume that understanding our children would come naturally. Maybe we assumed they'd be a lot like us, or at least that our careful nurturing would go a long way toward "molding" them into who they are. It is therefore often a shock to find out that your sweet little girl has her own and very different set of needs, curiosities, and interests. On the one hand, it's astounding to realize that such a tiny person can come so fully equipped with all the ingredients of a full-blown unique personality. But at the same time it means we now have to work (and sometimes work hard) to understand them with the depth they deserve.

The first part of the challenge is dropping all our preconceived ideas. We have to stop assuming, and instead watch and wonder. Listen to the things she talks about and is interested in. Try to track the threads that tie her youthful wandering thoughts together. Dig deeply into the whys and wherefores of her feelings. Try to remember what you were like at her age; try to imagine what it must be like to be her in this day and age.

Fit yourself in her shoes as snugly and often as you can and leave yourself open to who she really is. Chances are you will find traits you'd rather not find—maybe she has a hair-trigger temper, procrastinates, loves to play with spiders, or wants to be a police officer when she grows up. These may not be your preferences, but then it isn't your life either. Accept it, make your peace, and get on with the much more important job of knowing her deeply and loving her for all the uniqueness she brings to the world.

· ·

Parents: How is your daughter different from you? From what you expected? What are the traits she possesses that you might be less than pleased with? Can you see the ways in which those characteristics could be assets (for example, her willfulness might mean that she won't let herself get pushed around as you have in your life; her self-centeredness might help her put herself first).

Teachers: One way to rekindle compassion and understanding for your students' experience is to put yourself back in the learning experience. Study French, take an auto mechanics or computer class, anything that is new to you and preferably something that doesn't come naturally to you. Once you are experiencing the same kind of learning curve and difficulties that your students are, you will be able to empathize more readily.

· ·

Make home a haven.

"My mom was a frustrated interior decorator and she was forever redoing our house. For the most part I really liked what she did, but it wasn't until my junior year in high school that I was finally able to put my foot down and have the kind of bedroom I wanted. Until then I always sort of lived in my mother's version of what her daughter would love."

The world can be a scary place. It's hard enough when we are all grown-up and have to try to make sense out of things and find our place and purpose in the midst of all that clatter and confusion. Just imagine how alternately beautiful and wondrous and mysteriously terrifying it can be to a child without any of the resources necessary to sort it out. Yet that is the world we are raising them to live in. Therein lies one of the greatest challenges we face as caregivers—how to protect them adequately, to shield them from the full harshness of the world, while at the same time preparing them fully to deal with the world as it truly is. It's a difficult balancing act, but one of the key pieces that we can put in place without having to worry about whether we are overdoing it is to create a safe, secure, and supportive haven for them at home.

One part of that formula entails the conscientious elimination of any residual tensions—if you have an argument, if for any reason you need to discipline her, if there are any lingering issues between you that make your interactions uncomfortable, then you need to resolve them as quickly, compassionately, and supportively as possible. Get through the issues and back to what is important—your love and support for her—as quickly as possible. Home is no place for tension, uncertainty, or bad feelings. Without a solid foundation to build on it will be difficult for her to believe there is anything she can count on.

A second part of that formula is to try to help her make her own space within your home one that supports, nourishes, and reflects her emerging identity. This can require some tongue-biting at times, since the likelihood of your decorating ideas matching hers is pretty slim. But remember, this is her inner sanctum, the place she needs to feel most comfortable in, so go out of your way to be helpful and supportive.

· ·

Parents: What can you do to support your daughter's burgeoning sense of identity as it manifests itself in her room decor? Set aside a certain amount of money per year for a makeover? Stop nagging about the mess? Buy decorating magazines and dream with her?

Teachers: A classroom can be a pretty impersonal place, ruled over by the teacher. Look for ways you can allow your students to express their individuality creatively in their desks (if they don't rotate from room to room) or on the walls in ways that are meaningful to them (as opposed to posting assignments). Think about lamps, rugs, plants, even an easy chair or rocker that you could collect and set up together.

· ·

Get involved at school.

"My dad was the only father in my class who used to volunteer to help out on field trips, and it always made me feel special. Just the idea that he would take time away from his work to be around me and my classmates made me feel important."

By the time our daughter is school age, there is an understandable tendency to want to "hand her off" and be glad for the reclaimed time we can now apply to our own lives. It actually comes at a good time, when our daughter is just as interested in setting out on her own explorations, but it is very important not to go overboard. Not only do we have a responsibility to her to be her advocates and supporters in every way possible, but the kind of presence or lack of presence we exhibit in this crucial time sends a critical message. The girl whose parent knows little or nothing of her school life understands very clearly that her world is not a priority to her parent. It doesn't even rise to the level of interest—what a demoralizing and devastating message.

Conversely, being involved in your daughter's school can be extremely beneficial to her. Not only is it crystal clear that her world is a priority with you, but it opens a whole new area of dialogue. Does she have teachers who know her and respect her? Does she have friends? Are boys bothering her? Is she having difficulty adjusting to different teachers' styles? Be willing to discuss, intervene if appropriate, or assist if she is having difficulties with a teacher or a subject.

If there is an opportunity to volunteer at her school and you are able to do so, you will not only be helping out the school, but you will also be showing her just how important her education is to you. While this is hard to pull off when you are working full-time, the time you manage to eke out will be well worth it—for your own peace of mind and your daughter's well-being.

· ·

Parents: Is there a way you could make time to be at your daughter's school—even once a month for half a day? Think creatively—could you work half a day on a Saturday? Work one hour longer the rest of the week?

Teachers: Promote parent participation by encouraging their presence, helping them find the time, and giving them something meaningful to do when they're there. Get to know the parents of your students; their special skills and qualities might offer you something that would enhance the classroom experience.

· ·

Respect her privacy.

"My mother used to open my mail and go through the drawers in my room when I was at school. No matter how hard I tried to tell her what an invasion it was, she'd just laugh and say how interested she was in my life."

One day your daughter is crawling all over you, chattering away a mile a minute about the intricate details of her day, and then it seems the very next day she is becoming secretive and concerned about privacy. As she grows she will naturally begin to separate her life from yours. That much we can understand in theory, since the whole idea is to see her off into her own life fully capable and confident in her own abilities.

But the process can be difficult to endure. It usually takes place in fits and starts; one day we are confidants, and the next day we are excluded. Even very young girls who have just reached school age may be reluctant to share information with us about their new world, and the need for privacy only increases through high school. While it can be hard, particularly with a daughter who used to share everything, we must honor her need to experience and experiment with secrets and privacy, because ultimately she is practicing exercising her own judgment about what is hers alone and what and who will have access to different parts of her life. In other words, we might not like being excluded, but she is practicing becoming a strong, self-reliant, and self-confident woman.

Show your respect for her efforts by allowing her the privacy she desires. Allow her to designate which parts of her room or drawers in her desk are off limits to others. Support her if snooping siblings invade her domain, and unless you have a very good reason (grave emotional and bodily harm), discipline yourself to keep out of her private space.

· ·

Parents: Give your girl a gift of a box that can be locked as a concrete symbol of your understanding of her need to be in control of the parts of her life she shares with others. Tell her that you are willing to share any aspect of her life with her, but that you respect her right to have thoughts and feelings that are hers alone.

Teachers: Hold a group discussion about privacy. What is it? How important do kids feel it is to them personally? What are they especially private about: their space, their time, their belongings, their writings? With older kids, discuss the constitutional right to privacy—where should we draw the line?

· ·

Keep her secrets.

"I remember beginning to pull away from my sisters and mother when I turned thirteen. I knew I couldn't tell anything to any one of them without everyone knowing it all within a few hours. There was no such thing as a private confidence. Over and over I felt betrayed and misunderstood—it all happened behind my back, too. So I stopped talking to them. I never told them anything, and if I had to I lied about it."

A corollary of respecting your daughter's privacy is respecting her confidence. When she does share her innermost thoughts, fears, dreams, or desires, resist with all your strength the urge to share them with others without asking her first, no matter how cute, charming, or touching they might be. If you do, and she finds out (which almost inevitably happens), she will feel betrayed, and you will be cut out of a lot of conversations and confidences later on.

This is particularly a problem when she is very young, because the truth is that many times what comes out of her mouth is so precious you are just dying to share it with your mother, your best friend, and the mail delivery person. But if you do, you run a serious risk of embarrassing her in front of others. The wonderfully cute thing she said that you want to brag about can make her feel like her foolishness or immaturity is being paraded around to any and all willing to listen. It may indeed *be* precious and sweet, but children are understandably very sensitive to things that adults may think absolutely nothing of. The normal and wonderful process of growing up may be evident to us, but to her the humiliation of her six-year-old statement when she is now a big and mature seven-year-old can be extremely undermining.

Treat your child's confidences as you would expect a peer to treat yours. Never embarrass children. By showing her you respect her, you are showing her she is worthy of respect, nourishing her sense of her own self-worth.

· ·

Parents: When in doubt about embarrassing your daughter, ask her permission: "Is it OK if I tell Grandma about what you said to the neighbor when we took you trick or treating [or about the guy you just had your first date with]? I know she'd love to hear." If the answer is no, you've got to respect that. And if you forget to ask and she is upset, by all means apologize.

Teachers: Hold a conversation about secrets—what are they? Are some good and some bad? What would be examples of good and bad secrets? With older kids, discuss the ethical responsibility in holding a secret—should you keep the secret if a friend reveals she has an eating disorder, has been molested, or is contemplating suicide?

· ·

Teach her how to think for herself.

"My parents always claim I'm a good kid, that they love and respect me. But they are always telling me what to do. How can they respect me if they never let me make any decisions on my own?"

It's easy to think that caregiving means bossing around the children in our lives. After all, they know nothing (at least in the beginning), and by now, we know a great deal, so it is natural to assume that parenting is a process of telling what we know. But that tendency is dead wrong. Most of what kids learn they must experience for themselves, and to the extent they do comply with our advice, they are in danger of becoming kids with low self-esteem who can't make an independent decision.

According to Tim Gallway, who wrote *The Inner Game of Tennis* and *The Inner Game of Golf*, teaching a sport to someone is not about telling them where to look when they swing or where to put their feet. Rather, it is placing the learner in the environment and asking the right questions so that the learner can experience for herself what it feels like to look at the ball when she swings or what happens when her feet are at right angles to one another versus parallel. Coaching therefore becomes more of a process of inquiry than a lecture.

So what does this have to do with girls and self-esteem? Parenting and teaching are very much like coaching. The more we can avoid the tendency to speechify and instead ask our daughter good questions when she comes to us for advice or in the context of a conversation, the more she will actually create the inner framework for making healthy decisions in her life: "Do you like the blue or the red one better?" "If a friend came to you with this problem, what would you suggest?"

Instead of lecturing her when she does something wrong, ask her to reflect on the consequences: "When you hit Francine, what happened? How did you feel? How did she feel? What did you learn from that?" Instead of giving a lecture on good study habits, have her experiment with a couple of methods and then follow up with questions: "Do you do better on a multiple-choice test when you read the book two days before and then have a conversation with someone about it, or does it help more to take a walk first and then review at the last minute?" The more our daughters understand themselves, how they learn, and how they feel, the more they can make their ways easily in the world, brimming with the confidence such knowledge imparts.

· ·

Parents: Before your daughter goes to bed every night, spend a few moments together. Ask her to reflect on something she learned about herself that day. What was it? With little kids you may have to help them think of something, but remember—what's important is what she learned, not what you think she should learn.

Teachers: Have your students begin to pay attention to how they learn by keeping a study diary and to share that information with teachers and parents—Do they do best to read first and then have a discussion, or the other way around? Can they study best at home with music or in silence? At a desk or the kitchen table? For more information, see the book *Learning Unlimited* by Dawna Markova and Anne Powell.

· ·

Teach her to create healthy boundaries.

"When I was growing up, my two older brothers pretty much ran me ragged. Of course I adored them and looked up to them, and they took full advantage—getting me to act like their personal servant through a combination of ordering me around and then being sweet as candy if I started to protest."

Sometimes it seems that much of our energy as parents is directed toward trying to "civilize" our little darlings. We try to get them to share their things, cooperate with others, be a little more sensitive to the needs of other people, and generally act in ways that acknowledge that the world was not created for them exclusively. The downside, and one we must be vigilantly aware of (simply because it is so much a part of the socialization of young girls in our society), is the danger that we may be unintentionally teaching our daughters that it is their role to put aside their needs and their desires in order to satisfy others.

"Be a good girl and get your brother something to eat." "Be a nice girl and don't make a fuss when we go to the restaurant your father wants to go to instead of the one you want to go to." "Be a good girl and be nice to your Aunt Betty even though she treats you like you aren't there and adores your little brother." It's a slippery and insidious slope that is all too easy to go down and very damaging in the end, because the result is a young woman who does not know how to draw the line, who has never been trained and supported in standing up for what she wants.

This can be a difficult balancing act. It is important to encourage kindness and generosity, but it is equally important to help her to know when the line has been crossed from a gift of kindness to an act of servitude. Because the circumstances can vary so widely, there are no hard-and-fast rules to go by. The real difference is in her heart, and the only way we can help her to discern that line is to prod her into practicing: "What do you want to do and how important is it to you?"

Parents: When planning family events, from a meal to a vacation, ask what her prefer-
ence is, and then find ways to support her as often as is fair. Keep a sharp eye out for
situations where she might be giving up something important to her for the sake of
others, and engage her in a discussion about why. When a situation arises where
you can see she is obviously upset about not getting what she wants but is still trying to act like it's OK, intervene forcefully and let her know that when she feels that
strongly it is her responsibility to articulate her position as strongly as she feels it.

Teachers: Engage students in conversation about when it is appropriate to say no.
How do you know when you are being taken advantage of? How do you balance
being helpful with your own needs?

Make her aware of the possibility of sexual harassment.

*"When I was in junior high school a boy from the high school used to
hang around waiting for me after school. At first it was kind of flatter-
ing, but then he started trying to put his arm around me and rubbing up
against me and things. It went on for months before I finally got the*

courage to do anything about it, I just thought it was probably my fault somehow."

It is a tragic comment on our culture that the harassment of girls is so commonplace. According to a 1993 survey on sexual harassment in public schools by the American Association of University Women, 85 percent of teenage girls have experienced some form of physical, sexual, or verbal harassment in school, and 43 percent said it made them feel less confident. It is small wonder that so many girls have a lot of anxiety about the possibility of getting teased and harassed.

It's common for girls who are being harassed to be very passive about it and just take the abuse. The process of harassment can be seen as a reaffirmation of what boys and girls pick up on from the earliest age—that boys are dominant over girls, and girls aren't as strong; the message is about strength. In her influential book, *Schoolgirls*, Peggy Ornstein explains that "the sexual teasing, stalking, and grabbing merely reinforces other, more subtle lessons: it reminds [girls] that they are defined by their bodies; it underscores their lack of entitlement in the classroom . . . ; it confirms their belief that boys' sexuality is uncontrollable while their own must remain in check."

Since at its root harassment is about strength and domination, the best defense is to raise a daughter who is strong and willing to stand up for herself. Teach her the right to say, "Stop it!" At minimum, teach her to come to you if she is being harassed rather than just taking it, and assure her that you will help her find a solution. Depending on the situation, it might be effective for her to explain to her harasser how his or her actions have made her feel, but ultimately she needs to be absolutely certain in her right to be free of any and all harassment.

· ·

Parents: Alert your daughter to the possibility of harassment at school. Describe possible actions—jokes, touches, taunts—and urge her to come to you if she experiences any of these.

Teachers: Initiate a conversation about sexual harassment. What are the various types? Why is it hurtful? What should someone do if they are experiencing it in school? Breaking the silence will help girls believe they have the right to speak out.

· ·

Work through the silence.

"When my daughter was fourteen, she started to withdraw. It scared the hell out of me because I didn't know what to do and everything I did do seemed to just make the problem worse. I got really lucky, because I went to see this therapist who got me to see how my style of parenting was driving her away."

One of the most difficult bumps in the road for parents is when all of a sudden their daughter retreats into silence. The reasons can range from those that are minor and easily addressed to much more serious ones, and it is not always easy to figure out—especially since she isn't talking. The one thing we know for sure is that she has withdrawn from us, and that in itself is a problem.

The reason could be as simple as that she feels she is not good at verbalizing what she wants to say. Everyone has different communication styles, but this problem can come up easily in a quiet girl in a family dominated by big-time talkers. And it often initiates a vicious spiral downward. Maybe dad and older sister love to engage in spirited verbal battles at the dinner table, and younger daughter feels completely outmatched.

That starts her feeling inadequate, then down goes the self-esteem, and soon she is convinced she can't even express herself well, so why even try.

It can also be a sign of more serious issues, particularly if a family hasn't been communicating well for a while. She could be grappling with a serious issue—an eating disorder, drug problems, depression, sexual abuse—and feeling isolated, unsupported, and as if she doesn't have anyone she can trust or confide in. Whatever the reason, the severance of communication is a signal that can't be ignored.

The first thing we need to do is reflect deeply on our own role in creating this breach. It is sad to say, but such a complete withdrawal can even be healthy for her if in fact we were unintentionally undermining her sense of herself with our criticism, unrealistic expectations, or insensitivity to her feelings.

Once we have some idea of why we have been cut off, we can begin to repair the breach (often you won't be able to discover if there is a serious underlying problem unless you do reconnect, for she won't tell you). But it must be slowly and with extraordinary sensitivity. The last thing you want to do at this point is to confront her and force her back on the defensive. Instead you need to show her that you respect her decision to withdraw—temporarily—and offer her other ways of expressing herself and other people to talk with, which may not be as hard for her as talking face-to-face to you. Affirm your love and willingness to go through anything with her.

· ·

Parents: Be positive and nonthreatening. Talk to her about noncontroversial things first—foods, television shows, sports, colors, jokes (no teasing or sarcasm, though). Take a walk, play tennis, do anything that puts you together doing something she enjoys instead of "talking" about what is hard for her. Write her a letter or send her an e-mail and tell her this written space is sacred, that nothing will be held against her, that she can say anything she wants and you will never discuss it in conversation unless she wants to.

Teachers: Teachers can provide a wonderful alternative to parents when kids are going through hard times. Indicate your willingness to be there for anyone who might be in need, and go out of your way to make yourself available to those who seem to be in some kind of trouble. Offer to communicate in ways other than talking if need be, for example, e-mails, journals, or drawings.

· ·

Accept her choice of friends as much as possible.

"When my daughter was fourteen she brought home a friend with a pierced nose and lip and I almost lost it. I couldn't believe this was the kind of person she was hanging out with. Fortunately (probably out of shock more than good judgment), I didn't say or do anything stupid. It turned out that Sheila, the pierced wonder kid, was the smartest, sweetest kid imaginable."

At every age, friends are crucially important to most girls and often the people they choose to associate with are not high on your list of great friend material. Add to the mix popularity issues, in-groups, and cliques, and your daughter's friendships just might drive you crazy.

While this problem can arise any time, the adolescent years can be an especially difficult time. Girls' bodies are changing, hormones are surging, they have enough of a grounding to think about everything and not enough to understand much of anything, and they are operating under (often self-imposed) pressure to hurry up and become somebody. One of the most important vehicles for all this exploration is friends. So prepare yourself for a parade you just might not have expected.

Some teens go through friends as fast as they change clothes; don't worry, they're just doing their job as teenagers—experimenting and searching for their identity. Being capable of making friends and good at choosing friends becomes, at this time in her life, a crucial test of a girl's social abilities, and the last thing she needs is you telling her what a lousy job she has done. Unless there really is some risk (she's in with a seriously bad crowd, friends are getting arrested), take a few deep breaths and try very hard to be as nonjudgmental as possible (within reason).

In order to figure out if you should be concerned, get to know her friends as much as possible, and remember that appearances—thank God—aren't everything. If you perceive a serious problem, voice your concerns, but remember, particularly in adolescence, your disapproval may drive her deeper into the dreaded person's arms. Except in extreme circumstances (in which I advocate even such drastic action as moving to a better neighborhood or school), you would do much better showing her you trust her choices than trying to micromanage her social life.

· ·

Parents: To a certain degree, you can help nurture or starve your daughter's friendships when your daughter is young, but as she grows, you will have to count on everything you've ever shown and taught her to help her make her own good choices. The best defense against a bad social group is a strong internalized self-concept.

Teachers: Help kids become aware of why they have chosen their friends; do they have interests in common? Are they intrigued because they are so different? Plan group activities that allow kids to get to know others who might become friends. Go out of your way sometimes to acknowledge friendships that exist by allowing students to choose who they will work with or sit by in the classroom.

· ·

Teach her to scream when necessary.

"One of the scariest things that ever happened to me was when I was about fifteen and I was visiting the city with my father and brother. We were walking back to our hotel after dinner and I was lagging behind, taking in all the magic of the city, when all of a sudden this guy cuts me off and sticks out his arm around me to force me down a side street. For a split second I was stunned speechless, then I realized my dad was right down the block and I started screaming like mad. The guy took off and I think I was shaking for the next two hours."

One of the most difficult and painful tasks we have as parents is explaining to our daughters the degree and danger of sexually sick people in our world. Simply because they are female, young women are automatically potential targets for sexual predators, and they need to be both forewarned and prepared in a way that, rather than terrifying them, empowers them to protect themselves. They need good strategies for avoiding potentially dangerous situations and for recognizing signs of trouble. Unfortunately it is not just the "bad guy" out on the streets they need to be warned about, it can also be a relative or close family friend who starts by being affectionate and then slowly crosses the line into inappropriate touching.

Girls should be taught from an early age how to identify quickly and escape just as quickly from any threatening situation. A good class in self-defense is useful not only for the skills it can impart but for the confidence it can create. A girl who feels that she is not powerless and can at least begin to defend herself is much more likely to project the strength that might, in fact, get her out of a tight situation. It has the added benefit of bolstering her confidence that she is capable of taking care of herself.

Of course, you should always encourage her to come to you if someone is inappropriately touching her, assuring her that you will help her in a nonhysterical fashion. Your calmness is important—a twelve-year-old girl I know took months to tell her mother that her English tutor was molesting her because she was afraid of her mother's reaction.

· ·

Parents: Have her practice screaming and yelling as loud as she can. This may sound silly, but many girls are socialized to be nice and considerate, and may not have an automatic reaction to yell at the top of their lungs, even when that is often the best option available.

Teachers: Take the time to discuss in your class students' right to the privacy and control over their bodies. Let them know that there are unfortunately some people in this world who don't understand that, and if they are ever approached or touched in a way that they feel is wrong or makes them scared or nervous, a loud, immediate, and continuous protest is a healthy response.

· ·

Healthy Risk Taking: Creating Experiences to Help Her Spread Her Wings

The process of learning—growing and stretching the bounds of who we are—has a built-in positive feedback loop. With each new discovery, each lesson learned, we become larger and more complete than we were before, and we gain confidence that we can continue to grow and learn. The process itself is like a self-esteem escalator, moving higher and faster all the time. The more we can do, the better we feel about ourselves; the better we feel, the more we can do.

As adults, it is up to us to provide the context in which our daughters learn to take risks and have the kinds of experiences that foster healthy self-esteem. We can do this in many different ways, both by providing the experiences themselves and by creating the feedback loops by which they learn from their experiences. It is not enough just to preach and support our daughters, we need to create the circumstances that will allow them to stretch and grow with confidence. Sometimes this means prodding them where they may be hesitant to go, sometimes it means holding them to a commitment they desperately want to back out of, but always it means taking the time and energy to know them well enough to understand how far to push and when to let go.

Encourage risk taking in the stretch zone.

"I loved baseball, and in junior high I decided to go out for the school team. I got through tryouts, and the coach was practicing me at short-stop and second base, which I totally loved because you got to be in on so many plays. But after a month of practice I wanted to quit because two of the girls on the team were making fun of me. My mom gave me a pep talk I didn't want to hear and very quietly but firmly told me no way was I quitting. Good call, Mom—I went to college on a softball scholarship."

Learning experts have identified three zones, one of which we are in at any given time. The first is the comfort zone. Here we are doing what we already know how to do. Life is easy here, but there's no learning going on at all. It's a comfortable but lazy place. Second is the stretch zone. Here we are trying new things, so there's a bit of fear attached, but we know we are capable of doing them. We're challenged, but not overly freaked out. The third is the danger zone—here we're overstretched, over our heads. All we experience here is panic and fear that we can't measure up.

Obviously, most learning, and the enhanced self-esteem that goes with learning, takes place in the stretch zone. (Once you've mastered something, suddenly you're back in the comfort zone and need to find a new challenge.) For our daughters, that means that we need to help them find experiences that stretch their capacities, but not utterly create fear that they are going to fail, be laughed at, or be perceived as a "troublemaker."

If she overly fears failure, fears making a fool of herself, or worries too much about pleasing others, she might simply give up trying anything new—whether it is a sport, a musical instrument, or even reaching out to a new friend. That's why it's best for learning to take place in increments— you don't just let your youngster stay at a friend's overnight before she's spent first an hour with her at your house and her house, then an afternoon, then perhaps overnight at your house, then she's ready to go off.

The more we remember to find experiences in the stretch zone, the more our daughters will experience the boost in self-esteem that life in the stretch zone offers.

· ·

Parents: To encourage a girl who is afraid to try new things, work hard to create a safe atmosphere for learning. Is there anyone at home or in class who mocks or teases about her efforts? Sometimes all a girl needs is support from someone who will not give up on her, offering her the chance to excel by providing her with opportunities for new experiences under conditions that she feels are safe.

Teachers: In learning new skills or concepts, you might begin with a brainstorming session that allows your students to realize what they already know. This makes them aware of their comfort zone before you introduce new material or a more complicated skill that takes them into the stretch zone.

· ·

Show her how to set and achieve goals.

"My mom had this pad of paper tacked up on the wall in the kitchen and on it were written all the things she wanted to get done. She would check off things as she finished them and add more at the bottom. I was fascinated with that list and convinced my mom did more things than anyone in the world. My proudest moment was when I was seven and she added a column on the pad for me."

For children, life has a way of just rolling forward like one of those moving sidewalks at the airport. Time passes, events come and go, but with the exception of birthdays and graduating to the next class level, there are very few road signs announcing your accomplishments. "Congratulations, you just mastered the alphabet, or read your first adult book, or learned how to multiply, or learned you first song on the piano!"

Part of the problem is that from our children's perspective, from the moment they are born they are running at full tilt trying to learn all the things that it appears to them adults have effortlessly mastered. They are so focused on all the things they don't know and can't do, they hardly have time left to stop and appreciate what incredible accomplishing machines they have become. Yet, helping our daughters to see the extraordinary string of achievements they have under their belts is a great way to get them to see just how capable they really are.

For the most part, they aren't going to set goals for themselves and then check back in to evaluate how they did—they are entirely too swept up in the headlong rush to grow up. But that doesn't mean we can't help out, and we have a secret advantage—we know how incredible they are and what amazing things they can accomplish. So whenever appropriate, with small things like learning to tie her shoes, to making a cheese omelet, from school work to projects to sports, help your daughter to set reasonable goals and then be sure to acknowledge and celebrate her accomplishments. Girls who have goals and realistic aspirations, along with a plan for achieving those goals, are girls who have a good sense of their accomplishments, and girls who feel capable have high self-esteem.

· ·

Parents: Right now, ask your daughter what one thing she would like to accomplish. Then help her break it down into increments and create a timeline: If it is to dress herself, for example, break it down into socks, pants, shirt, shoes with help, shoes without help. Then create a chart with each category and mark off with a check, sticker, or star when she does each part. When she completes the whole task, don't forget a celebration!

Teachers: How much of your students' learning can they control? Can you allow them to set goals—daily, weekly, monthly, and then work toward them? They will be more motivated and feel more satisfied by accomplishing self-created goals than ones imposed by you.

· ·

Encourage well-rounded play.

"I was lucky to have three brothers because when we were growing up I was swept up in a mad swirl of boy play; we built forts together (yes, I had to fight for the right to use the fort even after I had worked on it as much as my brothers), built and raced soapbox racers, and played baseball and basketball into the late hours. Then in the privacy of my own room I'd talk to my dolls and tell them about my day."

Play is important because it is practice, but practice for what? Thanks to the wonderful people who stand behind one-way mirrors with clipboards and watch children at play, we know that in general girls' play tends to be about "being," while boys' play tends to be about "doing." Girls practice being caretakers with their dolls, tea sets, houses, and role-playing games, while boys fly off into competitive sports, wildly imaginative alien worlds that must be conquered, and building massive structures out blocks.

Both forms of play are important, but the balance in our culture is way out of kilter. Practicing how to get along with others is something boys should do considerably more of, and practicing conquering the world is something girls should be doing considerably more of.

The overall picture is too muddy at the moment for us to understand fully just how much of our children's play is biologically motivated and how much is environmentally induced, but what is clear is that the combined force of the advertising industry and our own deeply ingrained cultural bias play major roles in directing our children's play. When most commercials and children's programming shows girls dressing up, playing house, and engaging in relatively passive games, while boys are shown kicking balls, driving toy race cars, and banging around with toy tools, the message is pretty compelling. To grow up confident in their abilities to take on the whole range of situations they will encounter, our daughters need to start practicing, and that means playing.

· ·

Parents: For a week, watch your daughter at play. Does she spend significant time on activities that encourage independence and exploration, or are her activities mostly about relationships and interdependence? If the proportion is tilted in one direction or another, do what you can to inject the needed elements for more balance. Watch your selection of toys—does she have mostly dolls and stuffed animals, or does she also have Legos, challenging computer games, and puzzles?

Teachers: Encourage the girls in your class to play a wide range of games: computer games, kickball, hopscotch, Red Rover.

· ·

Allow for dream time.

*"My dad was one those guys that had every minute of every day orga-
nized. When I was little I didn't mind so much, but the older I got, the
more I had to fight to find my own time. I wanted to go out with my
friends or maybe even do nothing at all, and he had a 'family event'
scheduled. The worst were vacations. We did everything you were supposed to do, hit every tourist spot, and came home exhausted and oddly
unsatisfied."*

One of the most unsettling concepts in our culture is completely unstructured time. Most of us feel the need to fill all our time, even play time,
with planned activities, with no gaps to do nothing. Many of us are so
busy with work and family obligations that the notion of "free time" is
laughable.

There is much to be said for good planning and efficient time management, but everyone needs to fit large chunks of unstructured time into their lives. This is particularly true for our girls, who need time to dream, to "space out," to imagine their futures. "Doing nothing" is an extremely valuable lesson to pass on to our daughters because it opens them to the exciting and wide world of their own interior landscapes of thoughts, feelings, and creativity that will solidify their appreciation of their extraordinary uniqueness.

When our time is completely structured, right down to the "recesses," the only things that can happen are contained within the plan—the barbecue will be great or a dismal failure; the trip to Waterworld will be wonderful fun, marred by too much arguing, or just downright lousy. What is missing is the *unknowable*—what might happen, what could arise, if nothing is planned.

By introducing our girls to this wonderfully enticing "empty space," we are introducing them to a portal into their own hearts and minds, where whatever they think or feel can emerge and be played with. We are giving them the tools of inner exploration, which ultimately will be their strongest allies.

. . . .

Parents: Many family therapists are encouraging families to take seriously the notion of the Sabbath—one day of rest during the week. A full eight hours to read, to contemplate, to pray, to dream. If that seems impossible given all your schedules, aim for at least a day per month. Encourage your daughter, if old enough, to journal, to paint, to listen to quiet music. (And join her!) The more she develops a relationship with herself, the happier she will be in life.

Teachers: By trying to meet all the requirements, school time can get overpacked, but the brain doesn't work well that way. Try to allow your students quiet time periodically so that they can doodle, look out the window, stretch out, and listen to the inside too, instead of only the outside.

. . . .

Let freedom of expression reign.

"Like most kids, I grew up spouting the beliefs of my parents, but sometime when I was still pretty young, my father realized what was happening, and he started to ask me what I thought about things before

letting on what his opinion was. At first I didn't know what to say because I didn't have an opinion, then when I'd finally get around to mumbling something, half the time he'd take the opposite side just to get me to articulate why I felt the way I did."

This seems obvious—ask any parent if they want their daughter to grow up strong and comfortable with her own beliefs, values, and opinions, and nine times out of ten you will get an unqualified "Of course." And it isn't surprising that studies consistently show that children with high self-esteem are most likely to come from families that encourage freedom of expression. What is surprising is how hard it is in practice to create the space for our children to have different opinions and views than our own. It's easy to let them have their opinions when they mirror our own, but as soon as they start espousing ideas that are anathema to us, we tend to react quickly and overly forcefully.

Healthy families are careful to foster an atmosphere where everyone's personal opinions are respected, even if those opinions are not universally shared. Girls who feel free to express themselves without fear, judgment, or rejection are happier and feel better about themselves than girls who feel they have to censor themselves to fit in. Girls who are encouraged to say what they think, even if it differs from their parents' or teachers' views, are more confident, more socially secure, and less likely to be led down some garden path by peer pressure. So bring the First Amendment to life in your home!

· ·

Parents: Make dinner time family discussion time. Establish some rules: No mocking or shaming, no interrupting (kids need space to form their thoughts), and no judgments. Encourage the honoring of even the most difficult topics, the most challenging questions, and make sure the more quiet family members get a chance to speak as well.

Teachers: Set aside a few minutes at the start of each class for open discussion. At the very least, make it a weekly ritual. Lay down the law. Make it clear that your classroom is an asylum, a place where nothing you say will be held against you (at least during the designated discussion time). Give a little U.S. history lesson on freedom of speech.

· ·

Nurture her creativity.

"My creative side got squashed in kindergarten. Our assignment was to draw a picture from The Wizard of Oz, *and I drew what I thought was a pretty good Tinman. My teacher showed the class two pictures, mine and Betsy Reilly's. Betsy's was the example of everything good and mine was the example of everything bad."*

How many of us have a similar story to tell—an insensitive teacher or parent who squashed our budding creativity. One of our greatest human treasures is our imagination, our extraordinary capacity to reach into another dimension and pull out textures, concepts, sounds, shapes, designs, and stories that delight and enliven our lives. And what a tragedy it is that so many people are cut off from this gift because we foolishly and artificially separate people into a handful of "creative" ones, versus the rest of us.

Whatever you do, do not let your daughter lose her access to her creative side because someone else decided she couldn't draw or had no talent for the piano. Creativity comes in a vast array of categories, and it is our job to try to help our daughters find the places where they can tap into that well of wonder.

Whether it is through music, writing, painting, drawing, dancing, making puppets, performing, storytelling, imagination exercises, crafts, or other projects, simply being engaged in creative efforts gives our daughter the almost magical experience of bringing something unique into being that wasn't there before. This is the gift of creation, and our daughters get to experience the powerful feeling of being the creator.

Creativity is a fount of renewal for self-esteem because it is completely personal and individual. It is her experience, one that should never be judged or evaluated (and perhaps not even shared, because the point is not whether anyone else thinks it's good, but that it is a true reflection of herself).

· ·

Parents: Don't allow creativity to become performance. Teach your daughter that her creations are for her own satisfaction. Encourage her to express her creativity in whatever ways she likes and expose her to as many options as possible. But make sure that the teachers of these forms do not evaluate, but only encourage and offer practical advice.

Teachers: Watch your tongue when it comes to critiquing creativity! And foster the creativity of your students by giving them a wide variety of options for assignments. Can it be a song rather than an essay? A collage instead of a book report?

· ·

Practice creative imagining.

"My dad use to play this game with all us kids, where he'd sketch out a scenario that we were supposed to imagine ourselves in and then we had to come up with the solutions. Sometimes they were really practical and sometimes they were wild, but they were always fun."

Children have wonderfully fertile imaginations, and left to their own devices they will wander off into magically imagined areas just as easily as they will deal with the contents of the sandbox they are sitting in. But as parents we rarely challenge them to use their powerful imaginative capacities to help enrich their own resources for growing. If anything, we tend to put a damper on things by trying to get them to focus on the practical issues at hand. Way too much "Stop doing this. . . . And start doing that" and way too little "Imagine yourself in this situation; what would you do?"

The scenarios should range from the tiny to the expansive, from "What would you do if some boy kissed you and you didn't want to be kissed?" to "What would your priorities be if you were the President of the United States?" "How would you comfort a friend whose father had died?" to "What would the world look like if you could change one thing?" By actively creating hypothetical situations we not only give our girls a chance to explore life scenarios with minimal risk, to try out and learn about values and life strategies, but at the same time we support and honor their creative capacity and encourage their own trust and reliance on their imaginations.

· ·

Parents: Make it a regular part of dinners to go around the table and create hypothetical situations that everyone needs to answer, and let the kids be as much a part of creating the hypotheticals as possible. And remember, don't put the brakes on just because you get one of those horrible "Would you rather be burned to death or run over by a car?" questions. Even those can be instructive.

Teachers: Creative imagining can be integrated into just about any part of the curriculum with fantastic results. By getting your students to offer their own ideas and solutions instead of just relying on the materials in the books, you get them to stretch their minds and get invested in the lesson itself.

· ·

Help her deal with shyness.

"When I was in the fourth grade, I was so anxious about having to perform a solo recorder recital that I made myself throw up just to have an excuse to go the nurse's office instead of music class. Nobody understood that it would have been impossible for me to stand in front of all of those kids squeaking out the notes to 'When the Saints Come Marching In' without passing out from sheer fright. I would have rather eaten a bucket of worms."

Shyness can be a serious obstacle that can prevent your daughter from experiencing the wealth of positive feelings that comes from feeling a part of things and conquering new challenges. A shy child's social self-confidence and greater willingness to try new experiences can be developed gradually through a variety of affirming experiences that you can set up for her. But first, make certain her shyness is really a problem and not just a healthy part of who she is. The issue we need to pay attention to is not how shy she is or isn't, but whether or not she is satisfied and happy.

Some children are naturally quiet and content to play by themselves or with only a small number of kids they've known for years. If that accurately describes your daughter, then respect her decisions and don't try to pressure her into being someone she isn't. If, however, you can tell that her shyness bothers her—she really wants to go out for the team, but is afraid of making a fool of herself in front of others—and makes her unhappy, there are plenty of things you can do to help ease her into being more comfortable in social situations.

First, don't call your kids "shy" within their presence; it just reinforces that self-concept. Be vigilant about praising her when she does something socially appropriate. Brag about her to other adults in a way that shows you're pleased. Pay close attention to the basics. Really shy children fall behind in some pretty basic social skills—like knowing the rules of playground games, which of course only sets them up for embarrassing situations and further drives them back into a shell. Try gently and unobtrusively to provide little catch-up seminars for her, wrapped up in the guise of casual conversation.

· ·

Parents: If your daughter is shy, encourage her to interact with younger kids who will be more accepting of her. Babies do wonders for shy girls. Allow her extra time to warm up to new people and new situations. To help her find success and enjoyment at parties or other group functions, try getting her together with a friend beforehand and have them go together. That should be enough support for her to get adjusted.

Teachers: Pay special attention to shy children and work with them one-on-one. Be careful not to embarrass them or force them to participate in class. For a shy child, volunteering to speak in class or even answering simple questions when called upon can seem like unimaginable accomplishments. Let her write a note rather than verbalize her understanding of the material.

· ·

Encourage an interest in math.

"Somehow I remember knowing from a very young age that girls weren't supposed to be good at math. It always bothered me because I like math, but I never did do terribly well at it in school until the sixth grade, when I was taken aside by my teacher who said my test scores in one of those national aptitude tests showed that I should be really strong in math. He told me that his expectations were that I would do much better than I had been. Since then math has always been one of my best subjects."

How much is hard-wired and how much is culturally induced? When it comes to math ability, that is a question that may take a few centuries to answer. Right now, there is an interesting evolutionary argument that holds that since men were wandering around hunting, they developed a better "spatial functioning" by continually drawing and redrawing maps in their minds, while the women were working on communication skills back at the village.

Interesting, but all we really know at this point is that today, girls and women tend to be underrepresented in the highest levels of math achievement and overrepresented in the lowest levels. (Conversely they are overrepresented in the highest levels of achievement in communications skills and underrepresented in the lowest levels.) The practical problem with this gender division is that math skills have a dramatic and direct correlation to future income—the better your math skills, the higher your potential income.

Remember, statistics are exactly that, just statistics. There are plenty of girls who are math wizards and boys who can't calculate their way out of algebra, but it raises a significant issue that we should be aware of. At bare minimum, be careful not to reinforce the stereotype, and do what you can to encourage your daughter to enjoy math.

Parents: If your daughter appears challenged by math, spend extra time with her and try to make it fun, not just around homework time, but in the real world. Have her help you pay the bills, figure out budgets, calculate the tip at the restaurant.

Teachers: Learning should be enjoyable, and that is doubly important for math, since it has the potential to intimidate those who are slow to pick it up. Put extra effort into making math fun. Tell stories from history that show how math was used; give practical examples from day-to-day life, and go overboard to involve the girls.

Teach the importance of financial self-reliance.

"The argument I heard over and over again growing up was always about money—my dad controlled it and my mom spent it, and it became a sharp knife between them. Laying in my bed at night listening to their fights, I vowed I would always have my own money."

One of the most surprising findings of a recent study was that most young women in their late teens still believe that in adulthood they will be financially taken cared of by a man. One thing this proves is that cultural traditions die hard. Despite all the rhetoric and intentions of the women's rights movement, despite all the evidence, firsthand and statistical, that women cannot count on that support, and despite the complete incongruity of working to become a strong, confident, self-reliant woman who will then be financially supported by some guy, the dreamlike mythology persists. I suppose there are strong reasons for this lingering belief, but they need to be nipped in the bud not only because in most cases they simply won't be true, but because just hanging onto this fantasy will itself undermine a girl's self-esteem.

After all, you can posture and pronounce all you want about the equality of women, but if you are still holding onto an economic model that directly places men in a position of power and control and women in a position of weakness and dependence, it is all just an inauthentic, ineffectual bad joke. What you will get is not a young woman with high self-esteem, but a young woman who knows what she should be and also knows she is not measuring up to her own expectations.

· ·

Parents: Expose your daughters to the world of money and business as early and as often as possible. Let her know that women comprise 87 percent of single parents, yet only 5 to 10 percent receive alimony, and the average child support payment is $140 per month. If you have your own business, involve her directly. Talk to her about budgets, costs, and profit margins. Have her help out with the family check-book, paying bills, anything that will give her a hands-on sense of what it takes to live in the world, and let her know that one of the tasks, indeed one of the signs, of being a mature adult is being able to make her own way financially in the world.

Teachers: Get the class involved in making up what they believe a household budget would look like and guessing what kinds of jobs make what kinds of salaries; then match up reality with their estimates.

· ·

Encourage an entrepreneurial spirit.

"When I was little, I used to pick wildflowers and sell them at a stand at the bottom of our driveway. I loved every part of it—from finding the flowers to arranging the bouquets to making the sale. It's funny, because now I run my own business and I still love every part of it."

Historically, men have been more risk taking than women—and this has been true in entrepreneurial endeavors as well. While this has been changing in the past few decades (currently the fastest-growing business category is women-owned businesses), still the girls in our care need to be encouraged to take the risks that creating a business from scratch require.

Girls as young as six to ten years old are capable of running the time-honored lemonade and cookies stand, while girls in middle and high school can run baby-sitting cooperatives, lawn mowing services, and dog-walking businesses. Since the jobs available to most teenagers are low paying and dead-end, we should encourage our daughters to take their talents and use them to create their own businesses rather than working for peanuts at the local fast-food joint. Depending on the business, they will develop math skills (including costing jobs), organizing abilities, the rudiments of marketing, negotiating skills . . . the list goes on and on. Not to mention the boost to her sense of independence to be earning her own money!

Since futurists claim that in the future the average worker will be a free agent, creating her own opportunities and moving from job to job, experience in starting something from scratch and seeing it through will be skills that will be invaluable as she makes her way through life.

· ·

Parents: Help your daughter see the opportunities right in front of her. Do you live in a place that gets lots of foot traffic and would support a stand of some sort? Does she love young kids, and are there busy parents in the neighborhood who would like a Saturday drop-off baby-sitting service that she and her friends could organize? If she is old enough to drive? Could she use her shopping abilities to become a personal shopper for busy moms and dads? By assisting her in focusing on her strengths and the opportunities around her, you will be helping her to think about her "natural resources" that will help her throughout life.

Teachers: Think about business opportunities you can do with your students that can also be great learning experiences. Selling school supplies or preparing a special luncheon could give kids important real-world lessons as well as a grounded experience in math, nutrition, and social skills.

. . . .

Empower her.

"Both my parents worked, so I spent a lot of time during the summer at an assortment of summer camps. When I was seven my summer camp experience really sucked, and I guess I complained rather loudly and regularly about it. So when the next year rolled around I was all prepared to throw a fit if they tried to shove me in that lousy camp again. Instead, my Dad walked into my room and dropped a big stack of

*brochures on my bed of all the summer camps in the area and told me
to go through them and choose."*

Power is one of those words that gives us pause because it can be misused
so easily. All we need do is look around, and it is easy to see people close
to us as well as those in the public eye who have a burning need to exercise power and control over others. Conversely, there are plenty of people
who spend much of their time and energy trying to avoid exercising any
power at all simply out of fear of being held responsible for the consequences. It is a conflicted issue, but one that is crucially important to re-
solve if our daughters are to grow up in confident control of their own
lives. They must learn to be comfortable and responsible in the holding
and exercising of power, and the best way for them to learn these lessons
is to start early.

Each of us, even the smallest children, need to feel that we can influence
and have some degree of control in our lives. This sense of empowerment,
the opposite of helplessness, helps them to realize they can accomplish
their goals and be successful. To help them feel empowered, we must give
them opportunities to solve their own problems, we must entrust them to
make decisions and sound judgments regarding their own lives.

But it is important to see that their responsibilities are appropriate for their maturity level and that they have access to the tools that they need to succeed. By trusting them with responsibility, we are showing them that we have faith in their abilities. But it must be a real trust—you can't turn over the decision to them and then take it back if you don't like what they decided.

This is obviously a gradual process. Only you know when she is ready for each step. But remember, the more we allow our daughters to make the decisions that affect their lives, the better decision makers they will become. Like anything else, it takes practice.

· ·

Parents: Right now, given who and how old your daughter is, where can you let her have power and control over her own life? In choosing her own ice cream flavor? In buying her own clothes? In setting her own curfew? Are there things you are holding on to that you could reasonably turn over to her?

Teachers: Think about the ways you can allow students to have decision-making power in the classroom. In where they sit? In how they prepare for tests? In determining class rules?

· ·

Nurture uppityness.

"My grandmother always favored my cousin over me. I know it was because my cousin fit the stereotype of the good little girl and I was seen as too pushy because I would state clearly what I liked and didn't like."

We have come a long way in the battle for women's rights, but insidious double standards still exist. It is unfortunately still prevalent for assertive girls to be seen as "pushy," "selfish," and "insensitive," when the exact same behavior by boys is at worst just "boys being boys," and is more often seen as a sign of strength and confidence.

While our society has always rewarded boys for their capacity to assert their needs and desires and loudly voice their opinions and pronouncements, we have tried to pressure girls into becoming quiet, complacent caretakers who are always willing to put their needs and interests aside so they can satisfy the needs of others. We need to encourage our daughters to stand up for themselves and not be pressured into backing down. They need to have the tools to understand when comments like "Now, now, be a good girl," really mean "Stop asserting yourself because it's a girl's job to take care of other people's needs, not assert her own."

Our daughters need to be sensitized to this kind of very subtle but unfortunately pervasive kind of discrimination and taught to become downright uppity when comes to exercising her rights and asserting her desires. Assertiveness is healthy—when a girl is assertive, she can say what she wants in a way that doesn't wound or attack the other person. When you teach your daughter to be assertive, you are giving her the skills to say no to drugs, drinking, sex, or other harmful behavior without alienating her friends.

· ·

Parents: Teach your daughter how to be assertive in her communication. For example, "No thanks, Uncle Tim, I don't want to go on a hike this weekend. I'm spending the day with friends" rather than lying that she's sick, or saying she hates to be with him. Be sure to compliment your girl when she shows her pluck. Reinforce her self-confidence by affirming her rambunctious spirit.

Teachers: Expose your students to biographies of "uppity women" throughout history. Conari Press has a great series of books about uppity women.

· ·

Encourage her to form a support group.

"Sisterhood Is Powerful."

—bumper sticker

One of the things girls and women have always done better than boys and men is confide in and rely on their friends, who can be a strong source of support in building and maintaining girls' sense of self-worth. There is definitely strength in numbers, and the power they can bring to bear on any issue rises exponentially with support.

Regardless of the circumstances, good friends who understand and support your daughter can make a world of difference. It is a whole lot easier resisting silly conformist pressure from the "in group" at school if she has a few friends who also see how pathetic it really is. It's easier to stand up for herself when she is being teased or harassed if she has a collection of friends standing at her side, and it's easier to take risks and stumble when she has good friends who will laugh and cry with her along the way.

Recently there has been a movement to create mother-daughter support groups for girls making the transition from childhood into adulthood. These are wonderful ways for girls to get support from older women as well as from peers (and mothers report that the support is invaluable for them as well). Book discussion groups, groups that form specifically to do rituals around girls' first menstruation, groups to empower girls to set goals and take control of the lives—the possibilities are endless. One group I know that has meet for a year has decided that their seventh-grade daughters will chair the meetings, with adult help if needed. It's a great way to learn group dynamics, protocol, planning, and leadership.

· ·

Parents: If the idea of forming a group appeals to you, you might want to buy *Things Will Be Different for My Daughter* by Mindy Bingham and Sandy Stryker. They outline an entire three-year plan for girls in grades four through six.

Teachers: Would a support group of the girls in your class be helpful in dealing with harassment, body image, esteem issues, and other issues girls face? Interested girls could meet with you during lunch once a week. You would be there simply to provide structure and help establish ground rules for conversation.

· ·

Create equality between sisters and brothers.

"When I turned sixteen, my father bought me a brand-new car. My older brother had an older model that he had to buy for himself. That was just the way my Dad saw the differences between boys and girls. At the time I thought it was great, but after awhile I realized that what it really meant was he thought I needed the extra help and wouldn't have been able to manage it on my own."

We don't need experts to tell us what the effect would be on our daughters if we welcomed them into the world by telling them that we love them very much and believe in their capabilities, but they need to know that girls just aren't as important and need more coddling than boys. The sad truth is that through most of the history of our culture these are exactly the messages we have sent, and they persist today in ways we do not even realize.

In many families, boys are allowed to stay out later or are given more freedom (or breadwinning responsibility, as in the car example above) than girls their same age. Girls are assigned "domestic" chores that are closely associated with caretaking roles—washing dishes, cleaning the house, helping with meals—while boys are assigned more "physical" or "masculine" tasks such as taking out the trash and mowing the lawn. From the earliest books we read our children, through the dolls and toy guns we buy them and the sports and activities we assume they are going to be involved in, there are thousands of subtle opportunities to send messages of what we think of girls. We need to be very careful to send the message that our daughters can do and be whatever they want, rather than reinforce the idea that whole areas of life are proscribed for boys only.

In *Schoolgirls,* Peggy Ornstein reports that girls who are treated differently from boys are at a sore disadvantage when given different expectations and standards than their same-age brothers. This discrepancy can result in resentment, frustration, and narrow self-expectations in girls, and can lead to their joining gangs, dropping out of school, and worse. By establishing that boy and girl siblings are treated fairly, you send them both long-lasting messages of gender equality. Do your best to establish that rules are fair and differentiated by maturity and age, not gender.

· ·

Parents: Ensure that boys' and girls' chores take equal time. I've heard girls point out that it takes forty-five minutes to do the dishes, but only five minutes to take out the trash. Model gender equality among the adults in your household. Dads should be encouraged to do traditionally "female" tasks like shopping and cooking, and moms can set a good example for kids by doing car maintenance, plumbing, or other typically "male" tasks.

Teachers: Discuss the historical roles of men and women in our culture, and point out that in the past, when society required it, women became ironworkers, ship builders, and performed other very male-stereotyped tasks. The movie *Rosie the Riveter* discusses the issue in a way that middle-school and high-school kids can relate to. Invite women construction workers, computer programmers, and scientists into your classroom to provide role models and inspiration.

· ·

Help her deal well with dating.

"The first big dance date I ever had was my sophomore year in high school, and I was a wreck. I just remember feeling so stupid all dressed up in fancy clothes. My dad came in when I was fussing with last-minute makeup, put his arms around me, told me I was the most beautiful young woman in the world and that someday I'd look back at this night and smile. I don't know why, but it made me feel so much more relaxed."

Girls spend an incredibly large amount of time worrying about their relationships with boys, and their self-esteem or lack of it is rarely so evident than within the emotionally fragile realm of crushes, dating, and love. In the teenage and even preteen years, it's common for girls' self-esteem to be totally wrapped around whether they are attractive or desirable to boys.

For any parent to watch this unfold is so sweetly painful. Our daughters are beginning the treacherous transition into womanhood, and there is very little we can or should do to ease that transition. We cannot teach them the lessons they need to learn on their own, but we can prepare them by giving them a framework that they can return to when the need is strongest.

That framework is the understanding that their newfound interest in boys, that queasy, exciting, different feeling in their hearts, means that they are at the very beginning of a long and extraordinarily beautiful exploration. It is a journey that will reveal to them the deepest places in their hearts, that will help them to understand their own interests and desires in amazingly vivid detail, and that will teach them how to honor, love, and respect others.

If we can help them understand the magnitude of the journey they are just beginning, it will help them put their first trembling experiences into perspective. This perspective reminds them never to give themselves away—whether sexually or emotionally—to get love, and that no matter what happens to the relationship, it is not a measure of their self-worth. These are hard lessons for many girls, but one hopes that the foundation of good self-esteem you have given your daughter will see her through. Learning to say no, and to identify and get out of a bad situation are important skills in any social situation, but are key to safe dating.

· ·

Parents: If she's interested in someone, suggest that she pay attention to his actions and words—does he treat her with respect or does he belittle her? Do they have similar opinions and values? Does he respect women in general? She most likely doesn't want your advice, but if you feel you must offer it, ask for permission to give advice before jumping in and resist the temptation to ask whether your advice has been followed.

Teachers: Engage your students in a discussion about respect. Help students discover how they experience being respected and how they show respect. Make sure the discussion touches on the realm of dating.

· ·

Avoid rescuing her.

"Whenever I got into some kind of problem, my mother was always there with the answer. At first I liked it, but eventually I came to see that it never gave me a chance to figure anything out on my own."

We love our children so much that it is hard for us to see them suffer, if only for a little bit, in confusion or doubt. As soon as we see they're having a problem, we tend to want to rush in and fix it.

This is particularly true with girls, who, unconsciously at least, we see as more vulnerable than boys. Studies have shown, for example, that mothers on beaches let their sons roam further from them physically, while they try to keep their daughters right by their sides, even though neither child was out of eyesight. While it may be true that girls are in more actual danger than boys (sexual abuse, for example, is more common with girls than boys), it is also true that such hypervigilance does less to make our daughters safe and more to disable them—sending them the message that we don't trust their abilities to take care of themselves.

I'm not suggesting that we not supervise our daughters or let them roam around unattended. But what I am saying is that unless they are in actual danger, we should allow them to figure out the solutions to their problems, rather than running in with the cold towel, the Kleenex, or the replacement homework. When we say to them, "I know you can figure this out," we send a strong message of our belief in their competence. When we say "Poor baby, come here and I'll make it all better," what we're saying is that they lack the ability to resolve the situation and must be saved by us.

This doesn't mean that they might not require help in figuring out how to solve the problem. But it does mean that we put the onus for the solution on their capable shoulders.

· ·

Parents: Help your daughter problem-solve by asking useful questions. In *Things Will Be Different for My Daughter,* there's a great list: What do you think? (teaches her to be discriminating); Where do you draw the line? (helps her set boundaries); What do you want? (teaches how to know her own mind); How will you get it? (sets goals); How realistic it is? (separates reality from fantasy); and What will be the consequences if you do that? (thinking into the future).

Teachers: In issues of schoolwork or behavior, help your students find solutions to their own dilemmas. Support them in being proactive in handling missed assignments or in setting consequences for broken rules. Avoid rescuing them with too many second chances or quick solutions.

. . . .

Grant her the right to change her mind.

"My mother was constantly reminding me of what I said or believed two years ago. It was like a constantly renewing indictment and the message was absolutely clear. . . . 'When are you going to grow up and stop being so flighty?'"

It's common for girls to have major mood swings, change their minds frequently, have revolving interests, and new friends. That is just part of tasting life and trying out different ideas, attitudes, and roles. The frenetic energy that many girls have in preadolescence and the teen years is all a very healthy part of finding their place in the world and forging an identity, even if it can drive adults to utter frustration. Just remember, we're the ones having trouble dealing with all this quick-change artistry—for them it's a fun and exciting time (with a lot of angst thrown in to boot). So try to relax, open yourself to and involve yourself in your girl's whirlwind of a world, and you'll both be better off.

Help her sort through her ideas and experiences through active listening and by remaining scrupulously nonjudgmental. Support her enthusiasm for new interests; engage her in lively conversations that help her think through her ideas.

Acknowledge these signs of growth, and praise her for being open to new things and looking to make her life more meaningful. By encouraging her you'll affirm her growing spirit, and help her build self-esteem.

· ·

Parents: This is easier said than done—especially when she's just announced that despite the two-hundred-dollar ice skates she talked you into buying last week, she's decided she hates skating and wants to take up skydiving. If you feel reactive or catch yourself starting to negate her views, practice taking a deep breath, and say to yourself: "You have a right to have your own feelings and opinions. You are a beautiful separate and perfect being who has her own mind and her own opinions" before you make a response. This doesn't mean you have to let her skydive, but your willingness to let her have her own desires will help you forge a comment that both honors her and sets your boundaries.

Teachers: Plan debates on issues in the classroom where students must take turns advocating different sides, then discuss what they learned. Help your students learn how to explore options and how that can and will lead to changed opinions.

. . . .

Help her find her bliss.

"When I was a young girl, I found a wounded baby bird and nursed it back to health. It turned out the bird was a red-tail hawk and I ended up becoming the youngest hawker around. It was the most wonderful experience of my childhood. I still have a picture of me standing there with this beautiful bird almost the size of me sitting on my wrist."

Study after study has found that the single most important characteristic of people who feel happy and fulfilled in their lives is that they are engaged in doing something they are passionate about. Conversely, one of the hallmarks of seriously depressed people is a lack of strong interest in anything. Ironically, the incredible technological changes of the past fifty years may well be making it more difficult for children to experience that kind of deep engagement. Not only has the variety of "things" we can do expanded astronomically, tempting us to dabble in everything and never become really absorbed in one thing, but the culture itself has veered radically to prepackaged entertainment; growing up is becoming more and more a spectator sport.

Help your daughter discover what captures her interest: a new hobby, pursuing a special interest, starting a collection, practicing to become the softball queen. What the hobby or collection is isn't that important; it's the thrill of diving into something new that is all hers. She can revel in the delight of learning all about it, practicing it, and mastering it—crucial steps that everyone needs to learn in order to succeed in life. In collecting coins, earrings, bugs, dolls, *anything* really, a child gets a lot of gratification hunting for things, sorting and studying, storing, and owning them. She has the satisfaction of realizing she has an interest that is all her own, not one that she has to share with anybody. She learns important lessons of autonomy and self-determination, proving that she is developing uniquely.

. . . .

Parents: Support your child by acknowledging that her interests are important to her, whatever they may be. Show up to root for her at her games or events. If she's a collector, treat her collection with respect. Acknowledge the significance of her endeavor by helping to procure a case for her dolls or a box for her coins. Help her feed her interest in something new by making a visit to the library with her. Make it fun, a treasure hunt to look for books about Beanie Babies, stamps, or baseball cards—whatever it is that she's interested in.

Teachers: Why is it only in kindergarten and first grade that kids are allowed to bring in something for "Show and Tell"? Why must older kids leave their passions at the schoolroom door? Having a schedule of "Show and Tell" right up through high school creates rich fodder for discussions on current events, history, economics, science, art, music. Sometimes the older kids get far away from their passions in the rush to grow up. Have students "reminisce" about old hobbies, interests, and passions they've dropped and imagine what it would be like to take them up again.

· ·

Encourage reading.

"When I started high school, I got captured by mystery stories. The cool thing about it was that my mom was also a big mystery fan, so in the middle of this time when we really didn't have much in common, we had mysteries! She'd pass on books to me and she'd give me carte blanche to use her credit card to buy books as long as I passed on the good ones."

For most of the history of civilization, the mark of a person's accomplishment and status was largely measured by whether or not they could read. If you could read, you had access to all the information and knowledge in the world. If you couldn't, you were stuck in a prison of ignorance. That part is no longer true, since the roaring din of modern electronic media can serve as a gateway to some of that information, but what television and the movies provide in special effects and glitter, they lack in depth and breadth. So much so that the real danger is forgetting how incredibly shallow and one-dimensional most TV and movies are.

A study conducted by Kansas State University, polling over six hundred grade-school children, found that "children perceive poor readers as less friendly and less popular than good readers." Paul Rand, executive director of the Capable Kid Counseling Centers, told *Working Mother* magazine: "This perception may contribute to the correlation between poor academic performance and low self-esteem." Clearly, a love of books and an eagerness to read will contribute to a child's success in all aspects of life, including how she feels about herself.

The world of books offers such variety and richness, so much more opportunity for the imagination to soar, that, to paraphrase Mark Twain, the difference between reading books and watching television is like the difference between lightning and the lightning bug. Raising our daughters to be in love with books gives them a tremendous reservoir of possibilities at their fingertips. There are inspiring books that showcase different cultures, career options, and role models; books that serve as affirming mirrors to girls' everyday experiences; fantasy books that spark the imagination; adventure stories that engage her dreams; history books that reveal the influence and accomplishments of women throughout history.

· ·

Parents: From the earliest age, give your child books. There are cloth books, plastic books for the bathtub, and even chewable books for teething. Children as young as six months old will eagerly flip through little board books. Make reading a part of your daily ritual when your child is still an infant. Before bedtime or another quiet time, cuddle up in bed or on a comfortable couch and read and enjoy books together. It will become a cherished time for both of you. When she gets older, she can read to you!

Teachers: Often reading in school is required reading, not reading for pleasure. Set aside time when kids can bring in and read anything they want, even magazines. Create opportunities for sharing.

· ·

Watch for the squeaky wheel.

"My older brother used to irritate me no end, because any time I was talking he'd interrupt and say that whatever I was saying was the dumbest thing he ever heard. It always seemed like nobody ever noticed. I can remember having dreams about taping his mouth shut."

Recent studies continue to show that at school, boys consistently get more attention from teachers, often significantly more attention. The purported reason is the old squeaky wheel syndrome: Because boys are generally louder and less inhibited about causing a ruckus, they end up with more attention focused on "managing" their behavior, while the girls all sit sweetly at their desks.

No one has yet done a similar study at home, but it is probable that the results would be much the same. Certainly the stereotype of super-charged boys and demure little girls is proved invalid often enough, but the message is clear and familiar to anyone who has either grown up in a large family or raised more than one child—if you want to get attention, act up!

The implications are serious enough that we should try to keep this in mind on a daily basis. Remember, one of the most important things to our children (at least until they become teenagers) is our time and attention. If we are blindly being led down the garden path by our squeaky-wheel son while our well-behaved daughter is getting ignored, the message we are sending is doubly debilitating. Not only is it clear that for some inexplicable reason Mom and Dad love him best—after all they are always talking about him and with him and worrying about him—but not being good can get you the attention you want.

Watch, also, if you are taking advantage of your girl's willingness to be cooperative. A friend of mine realized that she was asking her daughter to do a disproportionate share of work because she was willing to help, whereas her son kicked up a fuss when he was asked to do the littlest thing. That's not fair to our daughter's good-naturedness—she deserves equity in attention and in workload.

. . . .

Parents: Is there a squeaky wheel in your house? Does a quieter, "good" daughter get ignored in favor of a talkative sibling or parent? For three days, sit back at dinner and measure the amount of airtime each family member takes. If it's consistently disproportionate, work on bringing the quieter members out.

Teachers: Make a point to spend special time, perhaps have lunch, with the quiet co-operative students. You'll be surprised at what you may not know about these kids' passions and interests, their thinking and feelings.

. . . .

Make success happen.

"For the longest time I thought I was a child prodigy at Ping-Pong because I could always beat my dad. It was years before I realized he was an expert at looking like he was trying as hard as he could and just barely losing. The funny thing is when I finally beat him fair and square, he thought it was the greatest thing in the world."

One of the activities my daughter enjoyed most when she was little was playing "Chutes and Ladders" with me. For a long time it used to drive me crazy, because this was a game of pure chance: you spun the dial, made your moves, and what happened, happened. It was therefore difficult for me to get at all engaged; just the sight of her running across the living room with the game in her hand and huge smile on her face was enough to make me want to run. Until, that is, I finally figured out why she loved this game so much—she could beat me at least as often as I beat her!

It was a powerful lesson for me. She wanted an experience of success in a world where it is hard for young kids to experience it. Success experiences are not something that most of us incorporate in our parenting, but we should. For accomplishment breeds the belief that you are capable of more accomplishment, and success breeds an attitude that you can succeed.

That's why we need to go out of our way to create situations that will give our daughters that heady feeling of success. Whether it is games, sports, schoolwork, construction projects, hobbies, it doesn't matter as long as it provides opportunities for genuine success; in fact, the broader the spectrum of success we can create, the stronger her sense of accomplishment will be. Studies from early childhood experiences to corporate settings consistently demonstrate that one of the most important criteria for success is believing you can succeed, and that the most important factor in believing you can succeed is having a track record of success. So start helping your daughter create that track record today.

· ·

Parents: Pay attention to the things she is good at and the things that challenge her, and by watching carefully and planning even more carefully, create the opportunity for her to shine. Play games she can excel at, ask for her help organizing the closet, planning a party, doing the bills, coming up with a Christmas gift for Grandma.

Teachers: Find ways to keep track of accomplishments on a regular basis, whether it's a weekly discussion about what everyone is learning and doing or a classroom goal chart. Break down the large tasks into smaller pieces so students can feel good about mastering the multiplication tables, or their numbers in Spanish.

· ·

Give her the technological education she'll need.

"My brother got a Nintendo game for Christmas, and I was really jealous until I snuck into his room and played with it for a few hours while he was at soccer practice. What a dumb game!"

Recent studies have shown that boys are more likely to be skilled in using computers than girls at most any age. The experts tell us this is because boys are most interested in and hence excel at computer games, and this extends into using a computer for schoolwork as well. Of course, what they don't tell us is that until very recently, virtually all computer games were designed by overgrown boys with a boy's interests in mind (which is of course why boys like the games more than girls do).

It's a wonderful example of how the more subtle issues of gender bias can cascade into deadly serious issues: guys design games for guys, which accidentally (no one is postulating a conspiracy here) turn out to be great early technical training for computer proficiency and give boys a head start in the computer skills that happen to be some of the most crucial work skills to have at this time.

As a parent, you need to work overtime to make sure you daughter does not get lost in the technological shuffle. Introduce her to computers early, and put a concerted effort into finding out what kinds of things on the computer interest her. There are the beginnings of girl-centric computer games and software emerging on the market, but until the field levels out, you will have to be diligent about finding them. Many of these are games with dubious redeeming value, such as dressing Barbie.

· ·

Parents: Try to bridge this gap by making a concerted effort to introduce girls to computer activities and games that are more likely to appeal especially to her.

Teachers: As this book was going to press, I read a study reporting that, in part be-

cause of the concerted efforts of teachers, the gender gap in the sciences is clos-
ing—with the exception of the computer sciences, where it is widening. The au-
thors recommended that teachers bring women computer programmers,
engineers, and other technical professionals into the classroom so that girls will
begin to see that they, too, can be at the forefront of this crucial technology.

. . . .

Encourage her to play sports.

*"I had so much energy when I was young, I just needed to be doing
something, and softball was my salvation. It allowed me to run around
and have fun and show other people as well as myself that I could be
good at something."*

The early studies of girls and self-esteem repeatedly demonstrated a pat-
tern of young girls feeling relatively good about themselves followed by a
massive plummet in self-esteem coinciding with puberty. Later studies attempted to identify the different kinds of things that had an impact on that
precipitous drop in self-esteem. They looked at family situation, income,
status, friendships, grades, popularity, looks—everything they could imag-

ine—and when the results were in, the one thing that stood out was a major and unexpected surprise: girls who play sports, particularly team sports, generally have much higher self-esteem than girls who don't.

The exact reasons are still pretty much theory; however, a few things stand out as obvious. First, when you are a part of a team, your contribution, whatever it is, is important and highly valued by your teammates, coaches, and fans. Second, team sports provide a very concrete and supportive environment within which to learn how to turn mistakes and losses into something to build on. You get the experience of working hard toward specific goals; your practice and improvement is publicly encouraged and celebrated; and you learn how to accept setbacks without taking it personally.

Additionally, and often overlooked, is that you get to become comfortable with the strength, incredible beauty, and capacity of your wonderful body, which provides a strong layer of defense against the onslaught of negative body image messages that young girls get besieged with in our culture. When you have seen, felt, and experienced your body turn on a baseball and send it flying, make a quick elusive cut on the soccer field, crush a volleyball, or hit a twenty-foot jumper, the power and grace you feel helps you dismiss the idea that you are supposed to look a particular way.

· ·

Parents: From the earliest age, help her develop her coordination. Encourage her to kick, throw, and catch balls. Bring her to women's games—not just the men's games that dominate on television. Expose her to team sports like basketball, softball, volleyball, soccer, and field hockey, but also other sports like swimming, gymnastics, sailing, track, or tennis. Help her consider what's out there by showing her what her options are.

Teachers: Help your students understand that their bodies are also an important part of the learning process. Provide active learning experiences, such as role-playing and hands-on experiments to help all learners find confidence in learning through their kinesthetic selves.

· ·

Take your daughter to work.

"I remember visiting my uncle's box-making factory when I was about ten. It was like this magical place with all these big metal machines that cut and folded huge stacks of cardboard into neat little boxes. I think it was the first time I ever really thought about where all this stuff comes from."

The annual "Take Our Daughters to Work Day" program (now called "Take Your Child to Work Day"), sponsored and founded by the Ms. Foundation, enables millions of adults to take their daughters and other young girls to their workplaces. This is a wonderful way for girls to see not only the variety of options out there, but also get a better sense of what actually goes on in the workplace.

This is important, because the way modern life is set up now, the adult world is so separate from the world of children that it is like a parallel universe. All the adults get dressed up in nice clothes and drive off to offices, shops, and factories, while children head off to another day at school with their friends. Children have little real knowledge or experience about what adults actually do at work all day, much less about the range of career choices and what might be satisfying work.

Encourage every girl you are in contact with to participate in this program every April, and trade off with friends so that they can expose children to as many different workplace environments as possible. A girl who has had more exposure to the working world has a head start on thinking about and becoming more comfortable envisioning her own future. It's a better orientation than having someone come into the classroom, because the girls actually get to experience the environments in which various types of jobs take place.

This is also the benefit, of course, of after-school and summer jobs, which also should be encouraged as a way for your daughter to get exposure to work and the sense of accomplishment that comes from a job well done.

· ·

Parents: Throughout your girl's childhood, make a special effort to introduce her to the adults you come across in your community while they are at work. Arrange for her to go to various worksites, not just on April 22, but several times during the year.

Teachers: Arrange with local businesses to bring your class in for a couple of hours to get a sense of various work environments: high tech firms, publishing companies, rubber factories—the list is endless. Tie it to something you've been studying in class—the invention of the printing press or the structure of the molecule.

· ·

Expose her to travel.

"When I was in high school, my dad took me and my brother on a three-week whirlwind tour of Europe. Each day we'd decide where we were going and what we were going to do. At night we'd pore over the map

and toss ideas back and forth until we came to a consensus; then off
we'd go the next morning. He also made us do much of the 'interact-
ing'—buying bread and cheese, pumping gas, even asking directions and
then trying to decipher what was said by gestures. Every piece of that
trip is so strongly etched in my memory, it made me realize that I could
go anywhere."

As adults, most of us love to travel and readily recognize what an incredibly expanding adventure it can be. But for many understandable reasons, when we become parents, we begin to prune our travel plans into smaller and more homogenized pieces. Yes, it is a hassle to travel with kids, and yes, the kinds of places we want to go and the kinds of places they want to go don't overlap too often, but we are making a big mistake if we simply cut back our outings or keep going to the same kinds of kid-friendly theme parks year after year. What we lose is a truly extraordinary opportunity to expose our girls to a whole different part of the world and a whole different way of looking at life.

Travel is not only a powerful mind-expanding experience in itself, but by breaking us out of our daily routine, it presents whole new opportunities for interactions and communications with our daughters that would otherwise not exist. Go camping, go backpacking into the wilderness, trace the path of the early pioneers, drift down the mighty Mississippi and tell tales of the heyday of river trade, visit the early colonial villages in the Northeast and revisit American history, trace the route of the Erie Canal, try to visit countries where English isn't the first language. Crack open the invisible boundaries of what "life" is supposed to look like, and let your daughter experience firsthand the vast richness of the world we live in. It will go a long way toward making her feel confident and capable of handling herself in whatever situation she might be in.

Yes, it can be a hassle, but with some good advance planning, a willingness to be flexible, and an adventurous attitude, travel will not only be incredibly rewarding but will result in some of the more memorable moments in your daughter's life.

· ·

Parents: Involve her in the planning of your trips. Giving her some say in what you'll be seeing or where you'll be going helps to invest her in the excursion. By giving her some responsibility for part of the itinerary, she will not only gain experience in doing research and making decisions, but you will also show her that you trust her and care about her involvement, boosting her self-esteem.

Teachers: Create a diverse curriculum with wide-ranging influences. Post colorful maps and posters from around the world. Include images of other cultures and traditions within your lesson plans. Go on field trips and involve students in deciding where to go. Have discussions about other ways of living, other kinds of ecosystems.

· ·

7 Having Integrity:
Living and Teaching Values

One of the most fascinating recent findings about self-esteem is that simply praising kids—that is, just telling them over and over that they are wonderful—does not build self-esteem. Rather, researchers have found, such comments have to be grounded in something real to affect self-concept: "You did a great job on the soccer field, Anna, the way you didn't get upset even though you missed the ball, but hung right in there and recovered well."

What this points to is the first characteristic of living with integrity: living from a consciously sincere and honest place, where the words we speak always deeply reflect the truths we feel. This is crucially important when dealing with children, because they have an unfailing "truth-o-meter" for phoniness, contrivedness, or just plain lies. In other words, if we want to affect our daughter's self-esteem positively, we must mean what we say, we must be explicit and true in our praise, and we must praise her with sincerity, so that it resonates with her.

The second characteristic of integrity is living from a place of wholeness and completeness, not slicing our lives into small pieces that can be presented or withheld to impress or manipulate. In a world in which more people are consciously or unconsciously playing roles than are actually living from their own deeply embedded truths, integrity is an extraordinary, powerful, and rare thing. When we embrace our own lives, expose the depth of our beliefs to our children, and then actually live our lives consistent with those values, we present children with an intensely valuable model. When we then let her know that we expect the same from our daughter, by encouraging and supporting her in discovering and developing strong values of her own, we give her a precious gift of immeasurable worth.

Remember that presents are no substitute for presence.

"My parents got divorced when I was eleven, and a friend of mine who had been through all this before told me that pretty soon my dad would start buying me lots of stuff. She was right, and at first it was kind of cool, but then I realized the more stuff I got, the less time I spent with Dad."

It's pretty common these days to find families in which both parents work full-time and feel so guilty about their lack of time with their children that they attempt to compensate by providing the children with lots of material stuff. It's an understandable impulse, and unfortunately your children will help draw you down this errant pathway since they love to get stuff. But that is not what they need, and it sends a very damaging message—that love is interchangeable with, and therefore can be bought, sold, and traded for, "stuff." When that's the message being sent, then suddenly your daughter's self-esteem becomes reduced to how much stuff she has and how good it is, and that is a formula that can lead only to disaster.

We live in a world that, for all appearances, values "stuff" more than anything, and it is essential that in our attempts to transmit to our daughters the things we truly value that we let them know, in words and in deeds, how absolutely and completely wrong that message is. If you ever find yourself searching for the perfect purchase to make up for your busy schedule, stop yourself immediately. The time you spend shopping would be much better spent with your daughter. And while we're at it, don't make a habit of "shopping" with your daughter as a way of spending time together; the message is way too mixed, and it's too easy to slide over into the ugly quagmire of love equals stuff.

Instead of presents, our girls need our presence, our honest and complete focus: I am here with you, not thinking about the chores I haven't completed, not worrying about work, not distracted, not preoccupied, not emotionally removed—just here in this moment with you.

. . . .

Parents: How much time do you actually spend in a day with your daughter when you are truly present? For a week, keep track of the amount of time. At the end of the week, ask yourself if it feels like enough.

Teachers: Have students practice presence with one another. Break into pairs and have one tell the other a personal story. The listener should try to listen fully, without interrupting or losing focus, for two minutes. (That's a long time!) Then without comment, switch. Come back into the full group and discuss what it was like.

. . . .

Teach a healthy respect for things.

*"I was hard on my toys when I was little, and one of the hardest lessons
I had to learn was that when I broke them they were gone. I remember*

*throwing a tantrum once that ended up with my favorite doll broken
into little pieces. I cried and begged, but I didn't get a replacement until
I promised to spend an hour every Saturday for a month helping Mom
with chores."*

Teach your daughters a healthy respect for the things we need and use in our lives. By understanding what kinds of things are important and useful and treating them appropriately, we can inoculate our daughters against the insidious cultural addiction to accumulating things and clinging to them as if objects were truly a substitute for human connection. Rather than getting your child a new toy to replace a broken one, try to fix it, or make an attempt to find a new use for it. If a preschooler breaks something purposely—say rips a book or damages a toy—don't leap to repair the harm. When she realizes the consequences of her actions, that she has to live with the torn book or the broken toy, she'll have learned a lesson about value.

To discourage a preoccupation with material objects, model that attitude for your girl. Reign in your own itch to consume for the sake of consumption. Treat the things you own with pride and care, teaching her respect for the things in your home that have special meaning for you, other than just simply monetary value. Because you use it only on special occasions, you show her that the bowl your grandmother gave you has meaning for you. By telling her the story of how you found that dear anchor lamp at a flea market in London, and through your caring for it and polishing it, you imbue that lamp with soul for her.

Parents: Here's a graphic exercise to show kids the value of money. Cash your paycheck one month and get it all in twenty-dollar bills. Then dole it out evenly to the kids. Then have them give back all of your normal expenses: so much for mortgage or rent, so much for utilities, so much for groceries, for gas, for car maintenance. They'll be amazed as the twenties melt out of their hands—and chances are they'll beg for things less often.

Teachers: Do an environmental analysis on an item that kids are familiar with—say, cardboard and plastic drink boxes. Go from raw materials all the way through waste disposal (don't forget advertising and transportation!) to show them how many natural resources go into every little thing we have (and what we have to do to dispose of things).

Avoid insincerity and backhanded compliments.

"My aunts used to fawn over me in such a way that I knew they didn't mean what they said. It was as if they had read something in a book about how to treat kids, but their hearts weren't in it."

Just as important as making sure that you are truly present when you interact with your daughter is avoiding that shadowy, "half there" state of insincerity. The "That's nice, dear" thrown over the top of the newspaper; the "How was you your day at school?" tossed off more as habit than real interest. Children have the capacity to consume untold amounts of our time, so it is easy to slip into "pretend response mode" when we put on the appearance of interacting with them but in fact are not at all engaged. The problem is that even though it is not intentional, the message being sent is that they are not deserving of our attention.

If you catch yourself slipping into this mode—and we all end up there once in a while—stop immediately and apologize. Explain that it is not a lack of interest in what she is talking about, it is your own problem, whether exhaustion, distraction, or preoccupation with some particular issue.

Also, be very careful about giving the gifts of positive words and then carelessly tacking on backhanded compliments. These are statements that start out positively but make a quick turnaround and end up doing more damage than good: "You look good, considering all of those chocolate bars you ate yesterday," or "I'll always love you no matter what size jeans you have to cram into," or "Great catch, how'd you do that?" The last place our daughters need to hear backhanded compliments is from us. To reaffirm their growing sense of self-esteem, they need messages that signal complete engagement, support, and unconditional love.

· ·

Parents: It's amazing how we get stuck in habits of relating to our daughters, even when we know better. Usually it's because we were treated that way ourselves as kids, and the patterns are deeply ingrained. This is where a spouse or loving friend can be helpful. Ask them to tell you if you have this problem.

Teachers: Make sure in giving equal time and attention to your students that you don't fall into saying things that sound pat and nonspecific, or that don't have your heart in them. Wait until you can sincerely find something positive to say; students can usually tell if you are "just saying that" to be fair.

· ·

Encourage her to be true to herself.

"I spent my junior high and high school years obsessed with getting, and then staying, in the 'in crowd.' I was so concerned with fitting in that I lost all sense of my individuality. I was halfway through a college I did not even like (but my best friend wanted to go to) before I woke up and realized I had been living someone else's life."

One of the most difficult tasks we face is helping our daughter live her life with a strong sense of personal integrity. It's a difficult task, because as she heads into adolescence, her concept of her "true self" is still only in the formative stages; because each year she grows, she is less and less willing to listen patiently to what we have to say; and because our replacement in terms of influence is her equally young and ever-changing group of friends.

We know that when a girl has high self-esteem, she doesn't waste time and effort impressing others, because she already knows she has value. It's implicit. But if she's feeling needy of the approval of others, she'll be willing to go to great lengths to get it. The desire to be part of a group, to fit in, is normal; the willingness to distort who you are in order to fit in, however, is a clear danger sign.

Watch for the kinds of compromises she appears willing to make, for signs that she is sacrificing parts of her true personality to fit in. In some cliques, it's not popular to be smart, and many girls "dumb down" to be one of the gang. Suddenly she may not want to play sports anymore, even though she loves it, because "cool girls" don't. Or she stops reading and starts watching a lot of TV (which she's never been interested in) so she can relate to the lunchroom conversation better.

This can be a very subtle and difficult call sometimes, particularly because it is natural for middle-school and teenage girls to practice putting on different personae as a way of developing their own identities. But if you feel that somehow she is doing it to fit in rather than from an intrinsic desire, trust your instincts. Chances are you are right.

· ·

Parents: If you feel that your daughter is compromising herself too much to fit into a group, initiate a conversation with her about these changes in a subtle, caring manner. Point out how you feel she has changed, and talk about how those changes have affected you both. Don't try to tell her what to do, since that implies she is unable to figure out what to do herself. It won't work anyway. Do show her you notice and care by talking about it an open, nonthreatening way. By showing her the respect you want her to exercise toward her true self, you open the door for her to find her own way back.

Teachers: Initiate a conversation about peer pressure. Why is it so important to do or say certain things? What does fitting in with a group gain students? What do they lose in the process? Have your students imagine a classroom where everyone did the same things, dressed the same way, and liked the same things.

. . . .

Take control over the remote.

"My daughter wouldn't just watch TV, she'd be fixated. I knew I had a problem when I can home late one day and saw her run to turn the television off as I came up the stairs, and then deny that she had been watching it at all (she was on a very generous two-hour-per-day allocation, which obviously wasn't enough for her habit). When I touched the top of the television, it was so hot it had obviously been on for hours."

Before we die, the average American will have watched a whole year's worth of commercials. That's just commercials—think of how much time we will have sat there watching all those dumb sitcoms with their canned laugh tracks. The average child watches over a day's worth of television a week. Even a cursory look at the messages kids receive from television programming and advertising should send chills down our spines. They tells us that all matter of things might happen, but don't worry, it will all get fixed in half an hour; that we'll be plenty happy if we just buy that one more "thing"; that pleasure is the highest good; drug and alcohol use is cool; sex is casual or violent or both; violence is glamorous and used by all heroes; and holding any deep moral beliefs is naive. And this is what we are letting our children absorb like sponges.

How weird is this when we have studies that show that these media-blitzed kids' self-esteem suffers if they don't have just the "right" brand-name clothes? It's been calculated that by the time a child is a teenager she will have witnessed thousands of murders and other heinous acts of violence on television. She's also bombarded with unattainable images of beauty and success through the super-svelte and super-chic models and actresses who are prominent in all programming. We have gotten ourselves so deeply addicted to television that even when we step back and see how incredibly damaging it can be to our children, we feel guilty about even thinking of pulling the plug.

· ·

Parents: It's difficult in today's "wired" culture to live free of media messages, but there are ways to lessen their impact. First, cut back your own television consumption as much as possible, and then strictly control and monitor the selection and amount of television your daughter watches. And yes, that means being willing to fight over it and hold your ground. When you do watch television, try to do it together and make it a participatory event. Watch your daughter's favorite show and ask her some questions when it's over: How are the women portrayed as compared to the men? Are they self-sufficient or needy, dependent or powerless? Are they in control of their lives or in the sway of others? Who's in charge? What do they do for work?

Teachers: Host a similar discussion at school about the class' favorite show. What are the characters teaching us about life? About male/female relationships?

· ·

Make growing up fun.

"When I look back on my childhood, I laugh! I laugh because my mother was such a card that she could not resist a single opportunity to

make something ordinary funny. I know I'm the only Irish kid alive
who had a mariachi band at her first communion party."

In the midst of all this serious concern over how to do right by our daughters, don't lose track of one of our greatest and most underrated human gifts—laughter! Growing up can be hard work. It certainly will be filled with lots of mistakes, embarrassing occurrences, and downright mortifying moments. It will also try our patience, fray our nerves, and test our wits. Far and away one of the very best tools to handle all this and come back strong is a willingness to take it in stride and laugh about it. By enfolding our daughters in a household that is always ready to laugh and have fun, we give them both the tools and the practice for building a strong resilient sense of self.

At the same time, you can help cut through the grousing and complaining kids do by making the things they are not thrilled about more fun. If they are enjoying themselves, they'll forget about their past experiences, fears, or preconceived notions about the task at hand. They also won't be so wrapped up in performance.

Besides making time together and doing chores more enjoyable, humor can also help diffuse a stressful situation and enhance learning. When a child is upset and frustrated, she has a hard time seeing past the immediate problem to realize it's not the end of the world. Seeing the lighter side of things can bring around a new perspective to any problem.

Being playful is essential to well-being and successful development. A child who is imaginative, with lots of playtime as well as good relationships with playmates, is a happier and more satisfied child.

· ·

Parents: If you're having a stressful day, everyone's cranky and not getting along, just stop a minute and put on some of your most favorite, upbeat music. Dance around with your kids. Laugh together, dance together, and you'll break the grouchy spell.

Teachers: Having a sense of humor and being able to make children feel at ease is a boon to anyone working with kids. Have a joke of the day, which you spring on them at unexpected moments. Check out *The Laughing Classroom: Everyone's Guide to Teaching with Humor and Play* by Diane Loomans and Karen Kolberg.

· ·

Be supportive of her changing body.

"It seemed like everything was fine, I was hanging out and having a great time playing with all the kids in the neighborhood, and then all a sudden my body started changing and everyone got weird."

Experts have concurred that beginning in preadolescence there is a profound change in how girls feel about their bodies and their self-esteem. Girls who had previously been fearless and unself-conscious, self-confident and strong-willed, seem to change drastically around this time. How you take part in preparing her and shepherding her through this time of great vulnerability has a direct effect on she feels about her body and changing self-esteem, which become intricately interwoven at this age.

Start early in helping her understand and deal with the changes and pressures she will go through. Some girls start asking about their bodies and sexuality when they are very young. Whenever these topics arise, know that how you handle these early discussions will have an enormous effect on how willing she will be to talk about menstruation and sex when she is older. Be open, enthusiastic, honest, and nonjudgmental, and you'll set the stage for good communication.

Give her lots of emotional support so she is better able to withstand the outside pressures from peers surrounding body image. A strong bond between mothers and daughters helps influence how girls feel about their body changes and nourishes their self-esteem. Create a special rite of passage for your girl around the traditional time of transition between girlhood and womanhood—whether it's when she first menstruates, or turns thirteen, or another time of your choosing. Show her you acknowledge this important time of her life by marking it with a special celebration that is affirming for her.

Fathers often become awkward and feel confused about how to act around their daughter as her body begins to change. One of the most typical responses is that they stop being physically affectionate. This can make girls feel like pariahs. Fathers need to try to maintain a strong level of physical affection but do so in a way that follows her cues for comfort level. It's a fine line that needs to be approached with great sensitivity and respect.

· ·

Parents: This one's for Mom: Go on a mother-daughter retreat to a hot springs or health resort. By focusing on the body and doing things like taking hikes, getting massages, and taking mud baths together, you'll be affirming this special time of physical growth and change together. Encouraging her to stay grounded within her body through athletics or yoga, and supporting her efforts to nourish herself through eating healthily and maintaining good self-care habits, are all ways of affirming her at this time of change.

Teachers: A good resource to use is *Changing Bodies, Changing Lives* (Vintage Books), which has excellent, straightforward information about bodily changes, sex, and relationships.

· ·

Be aware of the danger of eating disorders.

"When I was sixteen I spent two weeks in bed with a horrendous flu. I couldn't keep anything down, and by time I got back to school I had lost almost fifteen pounds. What was weird was that all my friends kept telling me how great I looked, and I couldn't help notice that the boys were doing a lot more looking than before. After a few weeks when I started gaining back the weight I had lost, I sort of panicked and began secretly purging after eating. That went on for almost three years. Looking back I still can't believe it."

One of the most dangerous things that can happen to a young girl is to develop an eating disorder. Even after decades of study, it is difficult to pin down specific causes for most eating disorders, but certainly a major factor is our society's history of valuing women primarily for how they look rather than who they are. When the size and shape of a girl's body become for her the deciding factors of whether or not she will be admired, desired, appreciated, and loved, then the door to devastating eating disorders has been opened. Not coincidentally, recent evidence indicates that the constant rounds of dieting that many girls go through can themselves lead to eating disorders, since they promote an obsessive and highly controlled focus on food.

The two most common disorders to watch for are anorexia and bulimia. Anorexia is a serious disorder in which sufferers essentially starve themselves to death because in their own minds they see themselves as overweight. The disease is fatal in around 10 percent of the cases, and does serious physical harm in another 40 percent of the cases. Bulimia is slightly more manageable when caught, since the girls who are bingeing and purging are usually aware of what they are doing and why. However, both disorders are devastating physically and are powerful signals of a self-image gone seriously awry.

One theory that is especially important for fathers to pay attention to is that the source of many eating disorders come from girls feeling that their fathers have abandoned them just as their bodies began to change. In fact, many fathers do withdraw from their pubescent daughters, not because they love them any less, but because they are unskilled in demonstrating their love to a daughter who is turning into a woman. Needless to say, our own awkwardness and unpreparedness for this amazing unfolding cannot be allowed to lead to such harmful results.

· ·

Parents: Teach your daughter early a reverence and healthy respect for food. The more powerfully grounded she is in healthy eating habits, the better. Don't ever use food as punishment or reward; food is sustenance and shouldn't be confused with anything else. Dads, find a way to make certain that your blossoming daughter knows and feels the love you have for her. If you can't figure it out, ask someone to help you. This is too important to ignore.

Teachers: Educate your class to the physical dangers of eating disorders and encourage girls to speak to a parent or other caregiver if they or someone they know is at risk.

· ·

Encourage her to keep a journal.

"I started writing in my diary when I was twelve and kept it up all the way through college. A few years after I graduated I caught my mother reading one of my diaries and I got so upset I tore them all into tiny pieces and threw them away. I can't believe now that I did that, I would so love to be able to go back and see the person I was then."

Life is an amazing and ever-surprising journey, and the better we get at understanding ourselves, at understanding the things that motivate and move us, the things that frighten and paralyze us, the things that charge us up and bring out our passion, the better we will be at making the decisions from which our lives will unfold. There are few better ways to begin teaching our daughters to see and understand the patterns in their lives than to encourage them to keep a written record of what is important to them. After all, many important people's lives have been chronicled in books, so shouldn't hers? And while that may sound like an exaggeration, it isn't—the message our daughter will receive is that her life is important and unique enough that we think it deserves to be recorded.

A secondary benefit is that journaling cannot help but improve her writing skills, and being able to express herself in writing is not only a powerful confidence booster but enormously beneficial for every kind of success in life. Keeping a private journal is a self-empowering practice for a girl, allowing her an outlet for strong feelings and a way to cope with difficult things that happen in her life. Journal-keeping helps a girl become more aware of her opinions and predicaments, allowing to her to get to know herself better. Self-reflection fosters self-understanding and improves self-esteem.

. . . .

Parents: From the earliest age on, provide your sweetheart with a notebook—first for doodling and drawing, and then for journaling. You can model journal-keeping for her by always keeping one yourself. Make it clear that journals are private property, and show that you respect her privacy by letting her know that you would never read her journal without her permission.

Teachers: Journal writing works well in school too, as a way to chronicle what's being learned and as a way for students to keep track of their learning habits—what they've discovered about how they learn best.

. . . .

Let her see that the future is half-full.

"My first organized baseball game, I was playing second base, and in the last inning a kid on the other team hit a really high pop-up in the in-field. I ran in and called for the ball and then dropped it—we lost the game. I cried all the way home. When we got home, my mom put her arm around my shoulder and said it was a tough break, but she was re-ally proud of how I called for the ball when the other infielders were hanging back."

Studies show that optimists live longer, happier, healthier, and more meaningful lives. However, many children cannot have a simple conversation without including comments that reveal a negative self-image, peppered with disclaimers about their abilities and disparaging insights about their view of their futures. It's not always clear where these self-deprecating remarks come from, but sometimes it's a way of protecting themselves from being criticized by others. After hearing comments like "You need to go on a diet" or "Why can't you get good grades like your sister?" they figure that if they put them themselves down first, others won't take jabs at them later.

Whatever the source, stop negative self-talk in its tracks whenever you hear it, because it's bad training and can begin a tragic downward spiral that starts with self-criticism, moves on to self-doubt, and then, if unchallenged, begins to undermine your daughter's sense of worth and value altogether. What you can end up with is a girl with very low self-esteem who finds it truly hard to believe that she is special or that she has worthwhile talents, and who has very high, unfair expectations of herself. From that seriously flawed perspective, she can never be "perfectly" satisfied with herself or the world and engages in a self-defeating cycle of failure and negativity.

It may sound overly simplistic, but optimism, like pessimism, is largely learned behavior, and by teaching our daughters early that mistakes are great lessons, not signs of failure; that obstacles can be circumvented or overcome; and that joy and disappointment are choice not sentences, we give them the gift of unbounded potential.

· ·

Parents: If you want your girl to be excited about the world she's a part of, the best thing you can do is be open-minded and optimistic about it yourself. For a day, become conscious of the kinds of comments you make regarding yourself, your family, your work. Are you generally positive or negative? Work on making affirming statements, not negating ones.

Teachers: Make a practice of asking your students, "What are you looking forward to?" You can do this on a regular basis, say, in preparation for the weekend, but then try to get them to think long-term as well.

· ·

Provide a moral framework.

"When I was a kid, I swore I'd never use those four little words, Because I said so. *But wouldn't you know it, now that I'm a parent they just come pouring out of my mouth."*

Certainly a crucial part of raising children is helping to steer them away from socially unacceptable behavior and teaching them how to get along cooperatively with others. There is also a good deal of more specific line-drawing that goes on: it's not nice to hit people, it is rude to interrupt when someone else is talking, and so on.

Unfortunately most of this "socialization" training is reactive and negative—our sweet little darling makes some social error and we intervene with a no, no, no! What is missing in this scenario is the moral framework that gives reason to the rules. Without that framework, the exchange is experienced by our children as chastisement. Even if they vaguely intuit that we may be right, the predominant experience is one of having been caught up short and read the riot act. This in turn engenders feelings of shame, guilt, failure, and even sometimes anger and resentment. We may get the message across by virtue of our authority, but the point has is lost and the process does more to undermine their self confidence and esteem than support it.

By taking the time to explain the reasons behind the rules in ways that are appropriate and understandable to their ages, we not only honor our daughters with the assumption that they are capable of understanding and acting accordingly, but we make it possible for them to see that this is not just a reprimand. Rather, we are trying to help them by giving them valuable information.

Rules and reprimands without well-articulated reasons appear arbitrary and an exercise of brute authority. The message is "I'm the boss, you're the kid, I have power, you don't." That message not only does nothing to help children understand the moral underpinning of your judgment, but it also undermines their own sense of power and responsibility. Simply by taking the time to explain our reasoning, we allow them to work on the framework of their own emerging conscience, and we reinforce their confidence that they are fully capable of doing so.

· ·

Parents: Often we say "Because I said so" because we don't know what else to say. It helps to think about these things in advance of the moment. Why shouldn't we interrupt someone? Why is fourteen hours of TV watching not acceptable? If we work through the scenarios in our own minds first, we'll be able to give answers that make sense in the moment.

Teachers: Consider the reasons behind all your classroom rules. Why must everyone be quiet during independent work time? Why can the kids use the bathroom only at certain times? Don't just announce the rules, give the reasons behind the rules. If you can't come up with a decent reason, then get rid of the rule.

· ·

Help her to consider others.

"My father took me on a business trip with him to New York when I was eight. While we were there he took me to this great toy store on Fifth Avenue and gave me the money to buy something for myself and something for my sister who was back at home. When we got back, Dad switched the presents. Needless to say my sister was thrilled and I was indignant."

Growing up is an egocentric undertaking. In part this is inevitable: our girls need to develop a strong sense of themselves and of their own desires and interests. It certainly should not be surprising, then, that they will at some point or another display behavior that is not only selfish but callously insensitive to others. Ironically, however, it is the girl who was always allowed to assume center stage, who always got what she wanted, and who was allowed to get away with just about anything that grows into the young woman with low self-esteem. Being deferred to, catered to, and coddled may have satisfied some self-centered childish need, but it leaves her without the experience, resources, or confidence to function outside that distorted cocoon.

Conversely, girls who are taught from early on that they are not the center of the universe, and that we all have a responsibility to be concerned about the people and world we live in, tend to have much higher self-esteem. This is not only because their childhood experiences of learning the limits, rules, and responsibilities more accurately reflect the experiences they will be faced with as adults, but because the very concept of being responsible for people and things outside of oneself is empowering. It is, in itself, a statement that you are needed, that your energy and your efforts are important to others and to the world at large. Indeed a healthy sense of social responsibility can be one of the most powerful components in building a healthy, self-confident personality because it confers a purpose that is larger than yourself.

. . . .

Parents: Everyone wants to be of use. Help your daughter figure out how her unique talents can be of use in the world, right now, not just when she's grown. Is she wonderful with animals? Perhaps she can volunteer at a wild animal rescue foundation. Is she a great swimmer? Maybe she can teach swimming to disabled kids. Give her the chance to contribute.

Teachers: Initiate a discussion of social responsibility. What is it? How can each member of the class contribute to the community right now? Brainstorm a set of ideas and encourage the students to act on them.

· ·

Support her with a foundation of faith.

"When I was in high school, my grandmother died. I didn't really know how to act. We had never been that close, and it seemed to me that even my father was not that close to her. After the funeral Dad took me out on a long walk and talked to me about what it had been like growing up in an internment camp during World War II and how his mother had held the family together by a sheer act of faith. We ended up talking about a lot things we had never talked about before, and somehow it made me feel closer to my grandmother."

There's an old saying that one should never bring up politics or religion at a dinner party, and there's something in that wariness that rings true for books on self-esteem and girls as well. Both are tricky topics, guaranteed to bring as many different ideas about them to the table as there are dinner guests. But having a faith, whatever it may be, and sharing that faith with your daughters is an important way for them to feel connected, resilient, and help them find real meaning in their lives. All of which add up to positive self-esteem.

When we look at the world our girls inhabit, it is easy to believe that the big questions like "What's it all about?" and "Why are we here anyway?" have very little to do with their daily routines. But this is not true. In some ways, because they understand so little and are at the mercy of so much, they are even more at the mercy of fear and anxiety about the unknown. A framework of faith can help to order and explain what seems random and frightening; it can free girls, give them a frame on which to hang their versions of the way the world works, and eliminate much anxiety from their lives. A solid framework of faith can also help them to be less self-centered and can provoke them to be more caring and helpful to others.

Children tend to model their beliefs after their parents', at least until adolescence, when they may feel the urge to break with the spiritual traditions you have fostered. If we stay true to the values behind our tradition and make it clear to her what those values are, chances are the values will remain, no matter what religious direction she ultimately goes in.

· ·

Parents: If you have a spiritual practice, by all means include your daughter (and no sending her off to church by herself while you stay home, as so many parents of my generation did). Discuss your beliefs regularly within your household. Talk about what you think and feel are our reasons for being alive, our purposes for being in the world, and what this implies about of our daily behavior. By verbalizing your beliefs you are teaching your children about you and fostering closeness and understanding.

Teachers: Engage your students in a discussion about what scares them about growing up in the world today, and what they trust in that helps them face those fears. This could lead to a talk about family, community, friendship, faith, and even self-trust.

· ·

Remember that parenting's a privilege.

"I had just finished yelling at my daughter for leaving her clothes draped all over the bathroom when the call came telling me that my sister's son had been killed in a car accident. I burst into tears, for my sister, for her

*family, for my poor beautiful nephew who would never get the chance
to grow up, and out of shame for being so petty and forgetting how
lucky I was."*

Being a parent is an overwhelming job. The preparation is lousy, the responsibility terrifying, the hours start off bad and get worse, the loss of
time to devote to your own interests and passions is unbelievable, the bat-
tering your own ego will take as you discover over and over again how
little you know is breathtaking. And if you expect gratitude for all those
years of providing, worrying, teaching, supporting, forgiving, and loving,
you'd better be patient, because you'll have a very long wait.

In the day-to-day unfolding of this task, it is easy to get grumpy and
resentful, to figuratively or literally stamp your feet, throw your own version of a tantrum, and demand obedience or at least silence and peace. It
is at times like this that we need to remember that being a parent is not a
job, it is an incredible privilege.

There is no more sacred undertaking than the care, support, and nurturing of a new life, and there is little we can ever do in our lives that will
approach the awesome impact that our children have on our lives. It is
easy to get lost in the minutiae, arguing over meals, bedtimes, television,

or pierced body parts, and lose track completely of the miracle that surrounds us. We get on our treadmill and are so focused on moving forward that we forget that every piece of our lives has been changed, deepened, and vastly enriched because of our girl's presence in our lives. While we fuss and become frustrated over her response to our entreaties and encouragement, we can forget how completely we have been remade by the lessons she has taught us.

What better parents we could be if were we able to hold this in our hearts when our patience runs low, when energy leaks away. Raising children is a privilege, one we should thank them for on a regular basis.

· ·

Parents: How do you renew yourself as a parent? A hot bath? A talk with a friend? A support group? Do whatever you need to continue on with enthusiasm, patience, and steadiness. Your daughter's life, to a great extent, is depending on you.

Teachers: Teachers can have an enormous impact on the lives of the girls they come into contact with, and teachers need renewal too. What do you need, right now, to recapture the enthusiasm for your role, the feeling you had as a young, excited teacher?

· ·

8 The Honor of Stewardship

A few years ago at an airport café I overheard a panicked conversation by two fathers who were desperately trying to figure out how to "manage" and "steer" their beautiful daughters safely through the turbulent teens. I left feeling great empathy for them, since it can't be done, at least not the way they were trying to go about it. Life is a bumpy road at best, and the truth is we have our hands full just trying to deal with our own potholes and sharp corners. It is foolish in the extreme to think that we are somehow gifted and talented enough to manage and control our daughters' lives as well.

Which is not to say there isn't a good and much more effective solution: Train your daughters early to become creative and responsible masters of their own lives. Empower your daughter to be an independent thinker. Expose her to the richness of life, and encourage her to sample what it has to offer, rather than shielding her in the name of protection.

Let her know that the only correct answer to what she feels, what she wants, what excites her, and what she wants to become is the answer that rings true to her. At the same time, remind her that the decisions she does make will have consequences, and that they too will be her responsibility. If we have done our jobs properly, by the time our daughters are in their late teens most of our work should have been done, and we should be able to stand back and watch the beautiful unfolding of their young adulthood, confident that they will make the right decisions for their lives, and that they will turn to us when they need us.

One of the most painfully difficult gifts we must give our daughters is the gift of freedom. And the irony is that if we do our part reasonably well and succeed in raising a daughter with high self-esteem, she will demand her freedom sooner and more completely.

The time will come when she is standing in front of us, ready and anxious to assume full responsibility for her own life. And when it comes, we will see her in all her strength and beauty, but we will also see her in her youth and inexperience. We will know in the deepest part of our hearts that letting her go will also mean letting her stumble and fall, letting her make her own mistakes—adult mistakes—and pay the painful consequences. And still we will let her go, even while a part of us wants so desperately to enclose her in our arms and protect her from all harm.

Ultimately, to raise a daughter with strong self-esteem is simply to provide her with the tools she will need to fashion her own life with clarity and integrity. It is no guarantee that all will be well, but it will allow her to respond with resilience when things go poorly. It is no substitute for the years of experience she must endure before the pieces of her life begin to assume the shape and depth that resonate within her, but it will stand her in good stead as she learns her lessons. It will not protect her against the turbulent storms of life, but it will help her negotiate the shoals and reefs.

All of this will be in our minds on that day we let her go, all of this and the miracle of what will come.

Acknowledgments

Thanks first and foremost to Jo Beaton, who compiled the research on girls and self-esteem that forms the theoretical underpinnings of this book.

Love and thanks to Daphne Rose Kingma, who has held my hand over twenty years of parenting; so much of her perspective has become so completely my own that it is hard for me to differentiate which are my ideas and which are hers.

A bow of gratitude to learning expert Dawna Markova, Ph.D., whose deep thinking informs a great deal of what appears here.

Thanks also to Virginia Beene Rutter, for providing the Foreword, and whose book *Celebrating Girls* was the inspiration for this one.

A bouquet of thanks to my educational consultants who provided feedback and in many cases suggestions for the teacher portion of the book: Anne Powell, educational consultant and co-author of *How Your Child Is Smart* and *Learning Unlimited* (who was gracious enough to gather other teachers' opinions and ideas as well), and Judy Blomberg,

Professor of Education at San Francisco State University, and an expert in girls and self-image.

My deepest gratitude to the hundreds of parents and kids who have shared their stories with me so generously over the years.

And, finally, a most inadequate thanks to Shelly for being the beautiful, courageous soul that she is, and for taking me on this most incredible journey.

Self-Esteem Resources

Abner, Allison, and Linda Villarosa. *Finding Our Way: The Teen Girl's Survival Guide*. Foreword by Queen Latifah. New York: HarperPerennial, 1995.

American Association of University Women. *Shortchanging Girls, Shortchanging America: A Call to Action*. Washington, DC: American Association of University Women, 1991.

Apter, Terri E. *The Confident Child: Raising a Child to Try, Learn, and Care*. New York: W. W. Norton & Company, 1997.

Bean, Reynold. *The Four Conditions of Self-Esteem: A New Approach for Elementary and Middle Schools*. Santa Cruz, CA: ETR Associates, 1992.

Bepko, Claudia. *Too Good for Her Own Good: Breaking Free from the Burden of Female Responsibility*. New York: Harper & Row, 1990.

Berends, Polly Berrien. *Whole Child, Whole Parent*. Foreword by M. Scott Peck. New York: Harper & Row, 1983.

Bethune, Helen. *Positive Parent Power: A Seven Part Programme*. Northamptonshire, England: Thorsons, 1991.

Borba, Michele, and Craig Borba. *Self-Esteem: A Classroom Affair. 101 Ways to Help Children Like Themselves*. Volume I & II. San Francisco: HarperSanFrancisco, 1993.

Branden, Nathaniel. *The Power of Self-Esteem*. Deerfield Beach, FL: Health Communications, 1992.

Braswell, Linda. *Quest for Respect.* Ventura, CA: Pathfinder, 1989.

Briggs, Dorothy Corkille. *Your Child's Self-Esteem.* New York: Doubleday, 1975.

California Task Force to Promote Self-Esteem and Personal and Social Responsibility. *Toward a State of Esteem: The Final Report of the California Task Force to Promote Self-Esteem and Personal and Social Responsibility.* Sacramento, CA: California Department of Education, 1990.

Calladine, Carole. *One Terrific Year: Supporting Your Kids Through the Ups and Downs of Their Year.* Minnneapolis, MN: Winston Press, 1985.

Campbell, Robert N. *The New Science: Self-Esteem Psychology.* Lanham, MD: University Press of America, 1984.

Clarke, Jean Illsley. *Self-Esteem: A Family Affair.* Minneapolis, MN: Winston, 1982.

Clarke, Jean Illsley, and Connie Dawson. *Growing Up Again: Parenting Ourselves, Parenting Our Children.* San Francisco: Harper & Row, 1989.

Clemes, Harris, and Reynold Bean. *How to Raise Children's Self-Esteem.* Los Angeles: Price Stern Sloan, 1990.

Curran, Dolores. *Stress and the Healthy Family: How Families Handle the Ten Most Common Stresses.* San Francisco: Harper & Row, 1987.

Curry, Nancy E., and Carl N. Johnson. *Beyond Self-Esteem: Developing A Genuine Sense of Human Value.* Washington, DC: National Association for the Education of Young Children, 1990.

Cutright, Melitta J. *Growing Up Confident: How to Make Your Child's Early Years Learning Years.* New York: Doubleday, 1992.

Dinkmeyer, Don, and Gary D. McKay. *Parenting Teenagers: Systematic Training for Effective Parenting of Teens.* Circle Pines, MN: American Guidance Service, 1990.

Erickson, Kenneth A. *The Power of Praise* St. Louis, MO: Concordia, 1984.

Field, Lynda. *Creating Self-Esteem: A Practical Guide to Realizing Your True Worth.* Rockport, MA: Element, 1993.

Hart, Louise. *The Winning Family: Increasing Self-Esteem in Your Children and Yourself.* Berkeley, CA: Celestial Arts, 1993.

Johnson, Carol. *Self-Esteem Comes in All Sizes.* New York: Doubleday, 1995.

Joseph, Joanne M. *The Resilient Child: Preparing Today's Youth for Tomorrow's World.* Foreword by Irwin Redlener. New York: Insight Books, 1994.

Koch, Joanne, and Linda Nancy Freeman. *Good Parents for Hard Times: Raising Responsible Kids in the Age of Drug Use and Early Sexual Activity.* New York: Simon & Schuster, 1992.

Kramer, Patricia M. *Discovering Self-Confidence.* New York: Rosen Pub. Group, 1991.

Leman, Kevin. *Bringing up Kids Without Tearing Them Down.* New York: Delacorte Press, 1993.

MacGregor, Cynthia. *Raising a Creative Child: Challenging Activities and Games for Young Minds.* New York: Carol Publishing Group, 1996.

Maderas, Lynda, with Area Madaras. *My Feelings, My Self.* New York: Newmarket Press, 1993.

McKay, Matthew, and Patrick Fanning. *Self-Esteem.* New York: St. Martin's Paperbacks, 1988.

McMahon, Tom. *Teen Tips: A Practical Survival Guide for Parents with Kids 11 to 19.* New York: Pocket Books, 1996.

Mindell, Phyllis. *A Woman's Guide to the Language of Success: Communicating with Confidence and Power.* Englewood Cliffs, NJ: Prentice Hall, 1995.

Mitchell, William, and Charles Paul Conn. *The Power of Positive Parenting.* New York: Wynwood Press, 1989.

Ornstein, Peggy. *Schoolgirls: Young Women, Self-Esteem, and the Confidence Gap.* New York: Doubleday, 1994.

Phillips, Debora, with Fred A. Bernstein. *How to Give Your Child a Great Self-Image.* New York: Random House, 1989.

Pipher, Mary. *Reviving Ophelia: Saving the Selves of Adolescent Girls.* New York: Ballantine Books, 1995.

Rutter, Virginia Beane. *Celebrating Girls: Nurturing and Empowering Our Daughters.* Berkeley, CA: Conari Press, 1996.

Samuels, Shirley C. *Enhancing Self-Concept in Early Childhood: Theory and Practice.* New York: Human Sciences Press, 1977.

Sanford, Linda Tschirhart, and Mary Ellen Donovan. *Women and Self-Esteem: Understanding and Improving the Way We Think and Feel About Ourselves* Garden City, NY: Anchor Press/Doubleday, 1984.

Satir, Virginia. *Meditations & Inspirations.* Berkeley, CA: Celestial Arts, 1985.

Steinem, Gloria. *Revolution from Within: A Book of Self-Esteem.* Boston: Little, Brown, 1992.

Strommen, Morton P., and A. Irene Strommen. *Five Cries of Parents: Help for Families on Troublesome Issues.* San Francisco: HarperSanFrancisco, 1993.

CONARI PRESS, established in 1987, publishes books on topics ranging from psychology, spirituality, and women's history to sexuality, parenting, and personal growth. Our main goal is to publish quality books that will make a difference in people's lives—both how we feel about ourselves and how we relate to one another.

Our readers are our most important resource, and we value your input, suggestions, and ideas. We'd love to hear from you—after all, we are publishing books for you!

To request our latest book catalog, or to be added to our mailing list, please contact:

CONARI PRESS
2550 Ninth Street, Suite 101
Berkeley, California 94710-2551
800-685-9595   510-649-7175
fax: 510-649-7190   e-mail: conari@conari.com
http://www.readersNdex.com/conari/